Leading the Culture Journey

Elevating ***Everyday Actions***
to Create ***Extraordinary Workplaces***

Leading the Culture Journey

Natalie Johnson

Rebecca Johnson

WILEY

Published by John Wiley & Sons, Inc., Hoboken, New Jersey.

For general information on our other products and services or for technical support, please contact our Customer Care Department within the United States at (800) 762-2974, outside the United States at (317) 572-3993 or fax (317) 572-4002.

Wiley also publishes its books in a variety of electronic formats. Some content that appears in print may not be available in electronic formats. For more information about Wiley products, visit our website at www.wiley.com.

Library of Congress Cataloging-in-Publication Data is Available:

ISBN 9781394408917 (Cloth)
ISBN 9781394408931 (ePub)
ISBN 9781394408955 (ePDF)

Cover Design: Jon Boylan
Cover Image: © Stafeeva/stock.adobe.com
Author Photo: Courtesy of the Author

Printed and bound by CPI Group (UK) Ltd, Croydon, CR0 4YY
C9781394408917_150726

Contents

Introduction

Rebecca

It is 1999. I am 25, fresh out of graduate school. I am working as a family therapist despite the fact that I took zero classes in family therapy while getting my Master's Degree in Mental Health Counseling and am woefully unprepared for this role in all respects.

I am sitting across the desk from my boss, a tall woman with big glasses whom I find intimidating on the best days and absolutely terrifying on the worst. She often speaks with a condescending tone and an expressionless face. I have seen her raise her voice in meetings and publicly diminish people's ideas. I do my best to stay under her radar, so she doesn't turn that type of attention on me.

Today, she is giving me feedback on a family therapy session I recently completed, which was recorded for the purpose of evaluation. Her feedback on my session is tough and not delivered with any care that I can feel. This feedback is delivered in the context of a relationship between the two of us that has never felt good to me. Today and every day, I sense she does not like me and maybe even has some sort of special contempt for me.

As she stares at me, I feel myself begin to well up inside. I try hard to fight back my tears, but I've never had the ability to stop a cry, so the tears come out anyway.

"Are you crying, Becky?!" she asks.

While she is technically asking me a question, I experience no curiosity in her tone and she doesn't give me time to answer it anyway.

"If you want to make it in this life, you better get your big girl pants on. It's a man's world out there and there is no room for tears. Come back here when you can talk to me without crying."

I am dismissed.

I go back to the office I share with two other young woefully unprepared therapists fresh out of graduate school. One looks at me with knowing eyes. The other keeps her head down. They know their turn is coming. We say nothing.

Later that day, I take my lunch break in the same way I do every day. I escape the oppressive, fear-filled building and go outside to eat my sandwich brought from home on a bench in a common area. After I eat, I walk the common space in circles. The conversation I have with myself is familiar because it's the same conversation I have with myself every day when I'm at work.

"I cannot do this any longer. Something isn't right. This isn't how it's supposed to feel. I'm not cut out for this. What am I going to do?"

During most of my working days at this therapy office, my insides are consumed with a swirl of uncomfortable emotions and confused thoughts as I try to do my best in a job that is too big for me under the critical eye of a toxic boss.

But on these lunch breaks, my intuition is clear. My inner voice yells loudly at me as I circle the commons.

After many months of this daily hell, I decide I can no longer take it and I vow to quit. Since I have had several jobs now that felt terrible to me, I assume that I must not be made for the traditional workplace. I assume that I just can't handle what seems to inevitably happen at work, so I'll need to find a different way to support myself.

I walk into Scary Boss's office the next day and give my notice. She says very little. I think she is relieved. I know I am.

Just two years into my work as a therapist, I throw in the towel.

As soon as I give my notice, I sign up for a month-long yoga teacher's training course in the Bahamas, which I finance by putting the entire $2,250 charge on my credit card even though I have no idea how I'll pay it off.

I am too young and unaware at this point in my life to understand how fortunate I am to be able to simply quit a toxic job without definite plans in place. I have minimal life expenses and no one else to provide for and a supportive boyfriend and parents who will catch me if I fall. I have the privilege of freedom and options.

Always the planner, though, it makes me nervous not to know what I'm doing next.

So I put all my mental focus on this yoga retreat. I get excited about having a transformational spiritual experience, learning to teach yoga, and eventually becoming a full-time yoga instructor. I will continue teaching fitness classes and personal training after the retreat for income while I build my yoga clientele and eventually create a successful business.

This plan seems appealing to me right now because I imagine that yoga instructors never have to deal with the anxiety I have experienced at work so far. No fear-inducing responsibilities. No harsh bosses. No stomach in knots every single day. Just kind, peaceful people with flexible bodies and strong hearts looking to make the world a better place.

As usual, the Universe has different plans for me.

The Status Quo

This younger version of myself did not have the knowledge or language to understand what was happening. I had never heard the phrase "toxic culture" or even considered workplace culture as a concept. I had not read the empirical evidence illustrating how powerfully one's relationship with their boss influences daily working experience, their personal well-being, and the version of themselves they bring to work and home each day. I didn't know how workplaces could feel vastly different depending on your relationships with colleagues, your ability to learn without judgment, and the degree to which you felt skilled and able to contribute fully.

My assumptions during these years were something along the lines of:

- having a "real job" means I will be somewhat dissatisfied
- it is normal for bosses to be mean or absent, and
- I was going to have to learn to handle the discomfort—or escape the "real" work world and support myself differently.

These are assumptions that many adults still carry today, and understandably so. Many people we meet through our work have daily experiences that leave them feeling frustrated, uncertain, diminished, anxious, undermined, and overwhelmed. Work depletes them and leaves them with little energy to be present and connected with the people and things that matter most outside of work. They assume that this is "just how work is," try hard to cope to the best of their ability, and long for the time when they don't have to deal with it anymore.

But it doesn't have to be this way.

Really! It doesn't.

From decades of professional and personal experience, mountains of evidence, and a heap of good fortune, we now know:

- While discomfort is a normal and natural part of everyday life as a human, work does not have to feel chronically difficult; in fact, it can be a place that provides comfort, safety, connection, and meaning
- While some formal leaders are in fact mean or absent, that is not "normal" or okay
- Great leadership is about service to others and requires high levels of self-awareness and emotional maturity
- It is possible to contribute fully professionally and still have energy left for what matters most outside of work (albeit with a strong commitment to boundaries and value alignment—but more on that later)
- We all have an impact on the conditions at work through our everyday actions

Maybe you know this already because you're currently working in an environment that feels good to you. If you're one of the fortunate few, for the most part:

- You feel cared for and supported by the people you work with
- You can contribute with meaning and purpose
- You and your team are able to navigate challenges well together, and
- You have energy left at the end of the workday to bring a quality version of yourself to the people and things that matter most.

But the reality is very different for many people—maybe including you. Can you relate with the experiences I just mentioned or opposite experiences? Check all that apply to you, either in your current role or past positions:

- **Your personal energy and well-being are negatively impacted by workload, dysfunctional relationships with colleagues, or other organizational dynamics:**
  - ☐ You experience chronic stress and don't see a light at the end of the tunnel
  - ☐ You're frequently overwhelmed or burned out
  - ☐ You have trouble focusing and experience a lot of multi-tasking and mental frazzle
  - ☐ You have the sense that you're "crazy busy" but still not attending well to the people and things that matter most
  - ☐ You don't get enough quantity or quality of sleep
  - ☐ You struggle to find energy or time to take care of yourself
- **The person you report to:**
  - ☐ Is under-skilled or overwhelmed and no one seems to be willing to hold them accountable to a higher standard
  - ☐ Is an absentee landlord, frequently not available when you need them
  - ☐ Is a micro-manager, diminishing your ability to contribute fully with the autonomy you have earned
  - ☐ Seems uncaring, distant, or classifiably toxic
  - ☐ Is a "nice person" but terrible at holding other people accountable or addressing situations directly
  - ☐ Makes the experience you and your colleagues have at work worse instead of better
- **You're part of a team that operates with a lot of friction, confusion, dysfunction, or drama:**
  - ☐ Your team members are superficially nice and polite with each other but lack the ability to speak candidly or address challenges directly
  - ☐ People on your team speak their truth quickly and easily but seemingly without care or respect for others
  - ☐ People on your team are exclusive, often openly valuing certain people over others

- ☐ Learning is difficult because you do not feel you can ask for help, acknowledge your gaps publicly, or admit mistakes
- ☐ Very few other people admit mistakes or ask for help
- ☐ There is frequent gossiping
- ☐ It is not common practice for people to challenge the status quo or healthfully dissent for fear of judgment or disapproval from others

While these challenges are human, normal, and common, *they are not inevitable*.

But they all have one thing in common.

You guessed it . . . CULTURE.

Culture 101

If you're reading this book, you either already know or have a strong suspicion that culture is important. You might already know that workplace culture affects nearly everything about people's experience: their personal energy and well-being, the quality of their relationships, their ability to contribute fully (or not), their ability to navigate and adapt to change, and the version of themselves they bring home after work. You might also know that culture deeply impacts an organization's ability to meet its financial and performance goals. Culture is the silent force behind how work feels and how well the organization can fulfill its potential.

Whether or not you already know the impact of culture, you probably want to be part of a workplace culture that supports you and others in working and living to full potential. You want work to feel better. You want yourself and your colleagues and your loved ones to feel better about work, at work, and after work.

The good news is that *no matter what your role in your organization is*, YOU can personally impact the culture you work in and the experience that you and others have. This book is designed to empower you to understand culture better and become equipped to positively impact it by leading or influencing the culture journey.

Before we jump in, here are few important things to know about culture—and what you'll learn in this book:

- **Every group develops one.** Any group of people spending a significant amount of time together will develop a culture. It's just what happens. Cultures are developed in families, on sports teams, in neighborhoods, even in friendships. And cultures are most definitely developed in workplaces. One of the perks of reading this book is its broad relevance. While you learn how to strengthen workplace culture, you'll also gain powerful tools to improve relationships and cultures you're part of outside of work.
- **Cultures can be accidental or intentional.** Most cultures are accidentally developed and not intentionally designed and nurtured. Because of this, most workplace cultures are mediocre at best, and some are classifiably toxic. Yes, there are workplace cultures that have not been intentionally nurtured that are "happy accidents." But these happy accidents usually only last for a short period of time because they are unable to maintain themselves as the organizational landscape evolves and adaptation is required. This book will be your guide for evolving your team or organization's culture from accidental to intentional.
- **In the workplace, cultures are very team specific.** If I were to ask you to describe the culture in your organization broadly, you might think "Well, which part of the organization? And from who's perspective?" This ambiguity is understandable because culture is most deeply experienced by humans at the level of the smallest unit. Instead, if I were to ask you to describe the culture on your team—say, your direct boss and the few colleagues you work most closely with—it would likely be easier to describe it. You don't need a big title to create change. You can start with the relationships closest to you and multiply your impact. This book shows you how to focus on your team and use that influence for maximum impact.
- **The leader of the team is the cultural architect.** Because of the inherent positional power of the formal leader of any intact work team, that person typically has the most influence on the team's culture and, thus, shapes how work feels and how it's experienced by others. If you are a formal leader of a team—meaning people report to you or

think of you as their "boss"—you have an extra set of privileges and responsibilities around culture. (Much more on this later.) If you're not a formal leader yet but aspire to be one, this book will give you a head start. Most formal leaders end up in their roles without awareness of their role in culture and struggle to lead people well. You can avoid those pitfalls by learning about the influence of formal leaders before you even become one.

- **Culture is everyone's business.** While the leader typically has the most positional power and greatest influence on culture, make no mistake: *every single person influences culture either positively or negatively through their everyday actions.* So, culture is ultimately everyone's responsibility. This is perhaps the most important lesson in this book. No matter your role, you have the power to influence change. This book will help you harness that power and become a catalyst for the culture you want to create.

Who We Are and Why We Wrote This Book

Before we go any further, let's introduce ourselves so you have a sense for who we are. You might know from the book cover that we are Rebecca Johnson and Natalie Johnson, co-founders of a workplace culture consulting firm called Vidl Work. While we share the same last name, we are not related. But we spend more time in connection with each other than with most other people in our lives! Here's a little more about us . . .

Rebecca

My professional life has always been focused on people; specifically, supporting others as they strive to transform into the next best version of themselves. This people-focused journey started in the early 1990s when I discovered Step Aerobics my sophomore year in college and quickly became certified to teach. (Think high top Reebok sneakers, big puffy socks, and mid-thigh length spandex shorts!)

Thirty years later, when asked a question I sometimes get from younger professionals—*How did you get where you are?*—my answer is often a rambling, twisty, turvy response including:

I followed my heart and my interests. I didn't have a master plan, but I paid attention to what was intriguing to me and moved in that direction with self-learning, certifications, extra degrees, and finding roles that allowed me to do what I was passionate about at that point, even if that meant I wasn't making enough money to be financially comfortable. (There were many years of not being financially comfortable!)

Over the last three decades, I have learned and served in many professional roles working as part of an organization that was owned and led by other people. I've worked as an individual and family therapist in a state-funded counseling center; the supervisor of a large employee wellness center; a health educator and program manager for an insurance company; and the director of employee wellness in several organizations.

At my core, though, I've always had an entrepreneurial spirit and most enjoyed the freedom of working for myself. In between and around my professional opportunities serving for established companies, I was involved in three entrepreneurial efforts prior to building Vidl Work with Natalie. In 2005, after discovering the then paradigm-shifting world of professional coaching and acquiring my certification as a coach, I started a private coaching practice. In 2007, I partnered with my dear friend Stacy to build an online streaming business offering self-development videos and content to the general public. Neither of these businesses endured, but they were exactly what I wanted to be doing at the time, and each was infinitely valuable in preparing me for my future. My third solopreneur adventure started in 2015 after I completed an extensive certificate program in Workplace Culture Consulting and started a private culture consulting practice, which was the precursor to the organization Natalie and I lead today.

I met Natalie in 2007 in the yoga studio owned by another dear friend of mine, Kiersten, where I was leading a weekend retreat mindfulness-based program that Natalie was participating in. I loved Natalie from the minute I met her. She has an easy, open, joyful, enthusiastic energy and she's one of those people that everyone is immediately attracted to. Natalie and I lived near each other and ran in the same professional circles, so we stayed in touch off and on for 10 years. Our professional journeys followed similar trajectories, as we both evolved from focusing on the individual to a broader interest in organizational wellness and then organizational development and culture.

In 2018, after several years trying to establish a successful culture consulting business and simultaneously working for someone else's organization (again), I realized I wanted and needed a business partner.

One thing to know about me is that I'm great at *doing* the consulting, facilitation, and coaching work, but I'm terrible at marketing my services and developing new business possibilities. I knew I needed someone who excelled in these areas. I also knew I wanted to have a partner with whom I could brainstorm, make decisions, and feel supported through the ups and downs of business. I was clear that I needed someone who already understood the work of culture and who would add her own set of unique strengths to mine to create a stronger combination.

With these criteria, Natalie came to mind immediately. There was not a single other person I would have entertained becoming business partners with.

So, in an uncharacteristically spontaneous move, I called her up . . .

Natalie

I've been an entrepreneur for as long as I can remember. I grew up in a health club and became a personal trainer and group fitness instructor in the 1980s. Both of my parents owned businesses, so creating my own business never felt like a risk. It felt natural.

Early in my career, I worked in nutrition and sport performance, where I studied how to help athletes train both their body and their brain. I quickly learned that the principles that work for world-class athletes are the same ones that fuel great leaders and high-performing teams. That realization stuck with me as my career evolved. I continued applying the same principles as my career shifted to working in resorts and studios. I worked with people who wanted to build energy and resilience for life, not just sport.

One of the most transformational chapters of my career was my time at San Diego State University, where I served in both faculty and staff roles. I didn't know it then, but it was my first real experience in workplace culture and leadership. Years later, I look back and see how much I learned about leadership, systems, relationships, and the invisible forces that shape how people work. I was in "culture school" at SDSU but I didn't know that yet.

Fast forward to the early 2000s. We moved to Florida, and I decided to try something new because I was tired and unhappy working in an academic environment (more on that later). During this time, companies were freaking out about healthcare costs, and they thought that investing in wellness programs would solve their employee health and cost problems. My job was to help them get results. After many years in this role, I saw the flaw in that approach. Employees weren't struggling because they didn't know they should exercise or eat vegetables. They were exhausted, unsupported, and working in environments that made it impossible for them to care for themselves. You can build a state-of-the-art fitness center, but it helps nothing if people don't feel safe stepping away from their desks to use it.

That's around the time I met Rebecca. She was also working in employee wellness. I don't remember the details of our first conversation, but I do remember thinking, wow, I need more of her energy. She had this calm, grounded energy that was so different from mine. Where I'm spontaneous, bold, and fueled by people and momentum, Rebecca is measured, reflective, and tuned into details. I asked her to help me with a few client projects (I was a solopreneur at the time), and it just clicked. She saw things I didn't, asked questions I hadn't thought of, and added depth to the work in a way that felt complete.

At the time, I remember thinking about how she was a single mom in a full-time job and saying more than once, "It's too bad we can't work together more." And then one day, years later, she called me.

Her company had been sold and her department eliminated. She was given the opportunity to take her department and client work and run it on her own as a business. She was hesitant. I had realized about a year prior that my own company needed rebranding and a new direction. But I had not done anything about it yet. The timing couldn't have been better.

I said, "This is it. This is our chance!"

We launched Vidl Work in January 2018—and from the beginning, we knew we were completely opposite. I live for noisy rooms, big ideas, fast decisions, and human energy. She lives for quiet spaces, thoughtful reflection, an organized calendar, and time alone or with her favorite people. If you ask us to describe a perfect day, we'll give you two completely different answers. But here's the magic: our differences *work*. They're our superpower. I love this quote from Adam Grant, Organizational Psychologist, because it describes us perfectly: "Great minds don't think alike. They challenge each other to think differently. The people who teach you the most are the ones who share your principles but not your thought processes."

We run our company, Vidl Work, using EOS (Entrepreneurial Operating System), which creates structure and keeps us on track. I'll admit, I don't like EOS. It forces me to slow down, focus, and follow a process. None of these come naturally to me. But I see the value, and Rebecca thrives in that space. Together, we're called "rocket fuel" by the EOS community. And honestly, that feels right. She's the solid, steady engine and I'm the blast that moves us forward.

We're living proof that people can build something powerful not despite their differences, but because of them. But that only works when you're intentional about how you work, on purpose, with shared values, and a commitment to the kind of culture you want to create together.

What You Should Know

Before we dive into the heart of this book, there are a few things you should know as a reader. First, you'll notice that we tell a lot of stories. Every story is true, but we've changed the names to protect their privacy. These stories bring the concepts to life, giving you a window into the very real challenges and transformations we've witnessed in workplaces like yours.

Second, we frequently provide resources like assessments, checklists, and tools throughout the book that you can download from our website. At the end of each chapter, we include a call-out box with the URL and the list of resources from that chapter.

Lastly, what we share isn't just the work we do with clients, it's work we live ourselves. Culture is not a destination, it's a journey. That's why we call our framework the CultureJourney®. The same practices and tools we rely on to sustain and nurture our own company culture are what we're sharing with you. Leading the CultureJourney means taking action as you read, using this book as a companion and a toolkit. So, let's begin; your culture journey starts right now.

1 Does It Really Matter?

An Executive Team in Crisis

It was the height of the COVID-19 pandemic, and I (Natalie) was staring at my laptop looking at a grid of small boxes. I was facilitating a virtual leadership training with the C-suite of an Ohio-based healthcare system. There were about 12 people in the virtual room, and their faces carried the strain of being in crisis mode. They faced daily staffing issues, critical supply shortages, policy changes by the hour, and the constant weight of leading teams through fear and exhaustion. We were there to talk about workplace culture: a topic that in normal times can feel optional. But this wasn't a normal time for anyone. From the moment we began, they seemed all in, asking questions, naming system issues and failures, and sharing frustrations they rarely had an opportunity to voice out loud. The more they spoke, the more they leaned into each other, and the training shifted from just another virtual training to something that felt really needed and necessary.

Halfway through, Jerry, their CFO, unmuted, leaning toward the camera. His voice was steady and also had some urgency. "Look, this is a good conversation," he said, "but we have to prioritize safety, efficiency, and accuracy, and we're drowning. This culture stuff sounds great in theory, but how do we know if this is worth the investment? Is there any proof it's worth it?" The digital room went still. It seemed like Jerry just asked the question everyone had been thinking but hadn't said out loud.

Is Investment in Culture Change Worth It?

Just like Jerry and his team, any person or organization that decides to invest time, money, and energy into an initiative should ask: "Why are we doing this?" Particularly for organizations, if the initiative doesn't serve a purpose, solve a problem, or meet an important goal, then resources would be better invested elsewhere.

Until relatively recently, it's been somewhat challenging to answer the question "Is it worth it to invest in designing and nurturing an intentional culture?" with empirical data and hard evidence. Culture has often been difficult to define, misunderstood, and confused with perks or morale and seemed too abstract to measure. But new research is emerging regularly and here's what we know:

If any of the following are important to your organization . . .

- Reducing turnover
- Improving engagement (which we define as "the degree to which people give discretionary effort")
- Reducing healthcare costs
- Improving the reputation of your company
- Maintaining or improving the physical, emotional, and mental well-being of yourself or your people
- Better leveraging diversity and increasing a sense of inclusion and belonging
- Innovation, learning, and navigating change
- Increased profitability and long-term financial health . . .

. . . then you need to pay attention to workplace culture.

The Research

There is a growing body of evidence supporting the fact that investing in workplace culture generates measurable results. Here are three examples of more recent research:

- Deloitte's 2025 Global Human Capital Trends Report found that companies with strong cultures saw up to 30% higher innovation, 40% better retention, and 21% greater profitability.[1]
- SHRM's global 2024 study notes that employees in organizations with good or excellent cultures are nearly four times less likely to seek new jobs, and more than 80% would recommend their employer to others—a clear indicator of enhanced retention and brand reputation.[2]
- A 2022 study by Charles and Donald Sull published in MIT Sloan Review[3] revealed two significant facts:
  1. The single best predictor of high turnover is a toxic culture.
  2. Toxic culture is *10 times more important* than compensation in determining whether an employee will stay with the organization or find employment elsewhere. Ten times!!

It's important to know that research on culture extends back decades. Another example:

- A 1992 study from Harvard Business School professors John P. Kotter and James L. Heskett[4] compared companies with strong workplace culture to those without. They revealed that over an 11-year period:
  1. Companies with strong cultures increased net income by 756%
  2. Compared to only 1% growth of companies with less effective culture

Your Intuition and Experience

While we've intentionally included empirical data that can help even the most skeptical person consider the value of improving culture through the financial return-on-investment lens, another way to consider the benefit of investing in workplace culture is to consider your own experience.

Think about the different places you have worked throughout your career and how each environment and set of co-workers empowered you or diminished you. Consider how some of your past work cultures have made you feel valued, while others have left you feeling incompetent, unnecessary, or "too much." Some have brought out the best in you and leveraged your strengths, while others have tried to keep you small. Some have energized you and connected you more deeply to purpose and meaning, while others have taken the wind out of your sails.

Those times you were feeling valued, competent, and energized? You were most likely working in a healthier culture or subculture that contributed significantly to your experience and that meant the organization benefitted from a better version of you. Those times you've felt excluded, undermined, micro-managed, or frustrated? Just the opposite.

Nearly every person we meet has had experience with culture that helps them recognize how it impacts them. Rebecca shared one of hers at the beginning of the book. Natalie's goes like this . . .

Natalie

It was 1998. I was sitting in my office at San Diego State University when someone peeked in, grinning, and said, "I'm just going to close your door." Not to block out sound for me, but to contain it, because my student staff and I were in my office laughing so hard we were in tears. That was normal for my office, the loud one.

I'd already done my morning loop, checking in with supervisors and peeking into fitness classes, before stopping by Eric's office, my boss and a campus veteran. I launched into the latest story about my student team: someone had turned a storage closet into a bed, complete with yoga mat and lights out and they were sleeping in it. Life in a brand-new campus recreation center was unpredictable, messy, and magical.

We were the first team, building something from scratch. A diverse group spanning generations, backgrounds, and experience levels, we managed hundreds of student employees who were enthusiastic but imperfect, sometimes oversleeping, showing up late, or causing chaos without meaning to. But our leadership team clicked. We worked hard, played hard, laughed loud, and leaned on each other. We shared advice, admitted mistakes, and celebrated everything from chili cook-offs to creative innovations. I won our creative innovation award one year and saved the department thousands of dollars. I used my award money to throw a party for the team. We always celebrated our wins. It wasn't perfect, but it was collaborative, creative, and full of purpose. It always felt like we were in it together.

And then, things changed.

The campus grew. Some of our team moved on or changed departments. Most significantly, a new boss arrived with a command-and-control style of leadership: his way or no way. The laughter faded. I stopped dropping by to say hello and instead avoided my new boss. I kept my struggles to myself. Meetings went from lively to cautious; it no longer felt safe to disagree or try new ideas. The thing is, no one intentionally decided to ruin the culture, but over a few years, our healthy culture slipped away like a song fading out. Eventually, I left the job I once loved.

As I look back on this experience, here's what I realize:

When culture changes for the worse, it rarely changes overnight. It erodes slowly, through small moments of what's encouraged, what's tolerated, what goes unspoken. Leadership sets the tone, often without realizing it. The same invisible current that makes a workplace feel alive can just as easily drain its energy. If we don't tend to culture intentionally, we risk losing what makes people love coming to work.

Your People Are Your Greatest Asset . . . or Are They?

You've probably heard that an organization's employees are its greatest asset.

From our experience, this adage is true, but only partially. What makes this idea *more accurate and concise* is to take it one step further to recognize this:

It's not just that an organization's people are its greatest asset. It's that the *relationships between those people* are their most valuable assets.

If you think about all the amazing accomplishments that happen in an organization that help fulfill the mission and meet strategic goals, *very few* of those things happen through the energy of a single person working alone. More often than not, greatness comes from people working together: collaborating, innovating, problem-solving, adapting to change, navigating different perspectives to get to the best idea.

Research by Timothy Clark[5] and his organization The Leader Factor indicates that organizational performance is enhanced when people in the organization can do four things together:

- Feel included
- Learn quickly (at or faster than the rate of change)
- Contribute fully
- Challenge the status quo

Think about these four ideas for a moment. These are not things people experience or do alone. They all happen *in relationship* with each other.

So the truth is this:

No matter what business result or key performance indicator you aim to achieve, or what strategic plan you have laid out, or what goals you want to meet, the most direct route to success lies in fostering healthy relationships among your team members. As you'll learn in the next chapter, *culture is all about relationships.*

2 What Is Culture and How Do We Change It?

Stacy

There's a popular story about two fish swimming. An older fish passes by and says, "Morning boys, how's the water?" The two younger fish look at each other and ask, "What's water?"

The point is simple. When you're surrounded by something, you sometimes don't notice it. That's also how culture works. Just like water, cultures come in varying degrees of health. If the water is polluted, the fish don't know it, because it's the only water they've ever known. It's only when they experience cleaner, less-polluted water that they feel the difference. In the same way, we often don't realize a culture is toxic until we've stepped into a culture that is healthier.

Stacy's journey is a powerful example of this truth.

Stacy was working as Vice President of an advertising agency when she started to realize something was off. From the outside, her life looked impressive. She was high achieving, driven, and moving at a relentless pace. She wore speed like a badge of honor. People told her she was a high performer, and she took pride in it. She even called it her "superpower." With every accomplishment she piled on more.

But underneath, the story was very different. Stacy says it felt like she was hovering above her own life, watching it race by in fast forward. The pace was constant, the pressure unrelenting. She wasn't fully feeling or able to connect with clients, friends, family, or even with herself. From the outside, she looked polished, confident, and in control. But on the inside, she was unraveling. She said it felt like she was drifting away from her life. What she had once celebrated as her "superpower" was actually her relentless drive to prove, perform, and perfect. And the cost was steep. It was draining her well-being, straining her relationships with her kids, and stealing the passion that had once fueled her.

This is what can happen when we're swimming in polluted water. Stacy's culture rewarded overwork, constant striving, and speed without pause or recognition. She worked on vacations, answered texts late at night and on weekends, and was even once sent on a wild goose chase to track down a UPS package at the airport. The company had no clear vision or shared purpose and everyone seemed to be chasing different goals. On top of that, favoritism ran deep, leaving her and her colleagues caught in an exhausting cycle of trying to earn a spot as "the favorite." This was the only water she knew, so she didn't know how toxic it was. It wasn't until she began to slow down and step into spaces that valued presence, recovery, connection, and authenticity that she recognized just how polluted her environment was. She had been swimming in polluted water for 17 years.

Stacy came back to herself by recognizing that the very thing that once fueled her—achievements and recognition—was also what disconnected her from what mattered most. Like the fish who only learns what toxic water is once it discovers cleaner water, she could finally see the difference between a culture that drains and one that gives energy. Today, she's no longer in polluted water. Her story reminds us that we can choose the water we swim in. When we choose fresh water, we create space to breathe, to connect, and to work and live to our potential. And as you'll read next, it's not only the quality of the water that matters, but also the way it moves around us.

A Rushing River

Workplace culture is perhaps one of the most misunderstood concepts in the modern business landscape. There are hundreds or thousands of existing definitions, but many miss the essence of it. This makes sense because culture is nuanced and complex and difficult to grasp—and even more challenging to change, especially among a large group of people.

We'll offer you a simple, seven-word definition for culture later in this chapter and we'll use that definition throughout the rest of the book. But, first, let's think about culture through the lens of a river, an analogy first shared with us by our friend and colleague Rosie Ward.[1]

Imagine you are standing on the shore of a rushing river. What would you actually be able to see or touch?

If the river is shallow enough, you might see the sand or muck on the riverbed. You might see rocks lodged into the shoreline that the water has to work around. You might see fish swimming or sticks floating by, or people swimming or kayaking. If it was breezy, you might see waves or white water.

What you wouldn't be able to see or touch is the *current* of the river. The current itself is invisible, but its force is powerful. The current of the river determines the direction the fish swim, the contour of the rocks, how fast debris flows, whether people can cross safely, and many other variables that you can't actually see or touch.

Thinking about culture like the current of a river is a good way to get a sense for it. Just like the current of a river, you can't see culture. You can only see the effects of it. You can't point to culture and say "That's it. Right there." You can't hold it in your hand or read it on a document. Like Stacy, we're experiencing the effects of culture powerfully every day without seeing it.

But despite its invisibility, it's tremendously powerful. Culture shapes nearly everything about the experience people have every day at work, the energy they bring to their personal lives outside of work, and the performance of the organization. Culture definitely shapes behavior. And, conversely, as we'll talk about shortly, individual behavior shapes culture. It's a cyclical relationship.

Seven Words

An internet search for "What is culture?" yields millions of results, so it makes sense that people are confused.

- "*. . . a collection of attitudes, beliefs, and behaviors . . .*"
- "*. . . an organization's unique 'character and personality'. . .*"

- "*. . . the cumulative effective that leadership practices, employee behaviors, workplace amenities, and organizational practices create . . .*"
- "*the official and unofficial rules . . .*"

To some degree, many of these definitions are true. They tap into a part of the essence of culture and are a great start for a definition.

While wordy definitions are okay for culture nerds like us who spend all day thinking about this stuff, we've learned we need to make culture simpler to think about for people who are interested in changing culture but less interested in needing hours or days to understand it. Not to "dumb down" the thinking around it or pretend it's a simple thing to change—but simply to give our brains jargon-free language to remember easily and use with each other.

So, we define culture through seven simple words:

The way we relate with each other

Out of the seven words in this definition, the most important word is "relate." At its essence, culture is about *relationships*.

Yes, transforming culture often requires changes in systems, policies, and processes. But we do not successfully change systems, policies, and processes without the ability to effectively relate with each other.

Culture on a Continuum

One of the many valuable insights that arose from the 2022 Sull and Sull[2] study is language to better understand what people are often thinking of when they're talking about a "toxic culture." Looking at more than 125 variables related to culture through the language of the people describing it, this study classified a toxic culture as one where the following patterns are normalized, or at least tolerated:

- Exclusivity
- Disrespect

- Unethical actions
- Cutthroat behaviors
- Abusive leaders

Now, you may look at this list and think: "Those are strong words. My organization isn't *that* bad." That would make sense too. Not all cultures that need attention are classifiably toxic. Some are just mediocre. Some are "fine." Some teams even exist in "nice cultures" where people are generally kind and pleasant with each other but so concerned with niceness that they are unable to productively disagree, resolve inevitable conflict, or get through the tension inherent in innovation.

When you gather data on the cultural experience of people in an organization, you'll often notice "pockets" of cultures that are team-specific: some toxic, some mediocre, and some very healthy. It's not unusual for a medium-to-large organization to have many, many subcultures within their organization that are vastly different from each other.

So while it's tempting to think about culture as either "healthy" or "unhealthy" or "good" or "bad," that's too black and white. In fact, most team cultures fall somewhere on this continuum (see Figure 2.1).

As you think about the culture on your own team, unit, or department . . . where does it fall on this continuum?

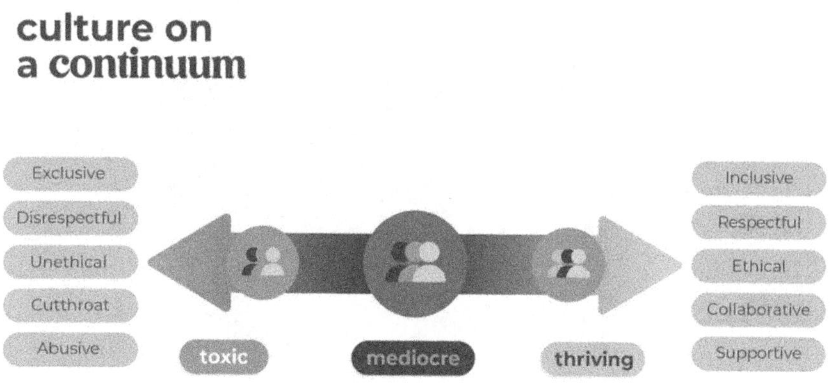

FIGURE 2.1 The culture continuum.

What Does It Take to Intentionally Improve a Culture?

We'll spend the rest of this book answering this question, but we'll offer a high-level answer over the next few pages so that you have a sense of where we're headed.

To understand how cultures change, we have to first understand where culture comes from and what it is "made of." In our work, we do this with a simple visual of four concentric circles. Culture sits in the outermost circle (see Figure 2.2).

Culture is the result, outcome, or manifestation of all the other stuff in the inner circles. But what's in those circles?

Just one layer in, we find "group norms" (see Figure 2.3).

Group norms are sets of behaviors that a group of people has agreed are valuable, acceptable, or at least tolerated. Often, this "agreement" happens without deliberate discussion or decision-making. We just accidentally agree that "this is the way we do things around here," even if the way we do things is not sensible, productive, or healthy.

FIGURE 2.2 Concentric circles with culture.

FIGURE 2.3 Concentric circles with group norms.

A good way to get the essence of group norms is to think about the last time you joined a new group of any sort: a new organization, a new department in your organization, a new sports team, a new community group, maybe you even joined a new family by way of marrying in.

When we join a new group, we often pay attention to the patterns of behavior we notice among the group members.

- *Do people hug here or is a handshake a better idea?*
- *What types of clothes do people typically wear?*
- *Do people take a break from work and eat lunch somewhere else or are most people eating on the go or at their desk?*
- *Is it good to be openly warm and welcoming here or do people keep it "cool" and distant?*
- *Do I hear anyone else asking for help or admitting mistakes or are most people acting like they have it all handled?*

A norm is a pattern of behavior we observe among most people in the group. We pay strong attention to norms to determine how we "should" or will act with others, even though we're often not consciously aware that we are doing so.

The table includes a few examples of group norms we've experienced in our work with clients. On the left are norms that are more likely to develop by accident and contribute to mediocrity or toxicity. On the right there are norms that are more likely to develop with intention and that are also more likely to contribute to or be a sign of a healthier culture.

As you read through this list of unhelpful and helpful norms, can you relate to any of them?

Unhelpful norms often found in accidental cultures	Helpful norms often found in intentional cultures
In meetings, the people in the highest positions talk the most. Other people don't offer very much input or feedback unless directly asked.	In meetings, listening intently and asking good questions is encouraged and valued no matter what role you are in. We usually have lively conversations.
People don't often admit mistakes or gaps in knowledge. They might be viewed as incompetent if they did.	People seem to feel safe saying "I don't know" or admitting mistakes because those moments are seen through the lens of learning rather than incompetence.
When people are out sick or on vacation, they still check and send emails. It feels like "always connected" is a status symbol.	When people take time off from work, they disconnect. Our culture encourages us to use our time away to fully recharge.
Our workloads feel unreasonable and no one seems to be able or willing to do anything about it.	When our workloads become unreasonable, we talk about it together. Leaders acknowledge the situation and adjust where possible.
When someone demonstrates bias or makes exclusive or derogatory statements, we stay quiet in the moment and talk about it behind their back.	When someone demonstrates bias or makes exclusive or derogatory statements, we assume best intent and have candid conversations to address the situation openly and learn.

In very practical terms, changing culture is about shifting people's shared patterns of behavior so there are less *accidental, unhelpful,* and *unproductive* norms and more *intentional, helpful,* and *productive* norms.

So the first answer to "How do we change culture?" is: **changing culture requires changing group norms.**

How Do We Change Group Norms?

Since group norms are sums of individual behaviors, it's logical to assume that changing culture requires changing the behaviors of the individuals in the group.

This is true. Any group that is going to change its culture will need many of the people within that group to change the way they *behave in relationship to each other*, at least a little bit.

For example, let's say you and your team decide to shift the accidental norms that have developed around communication overload and mental focus. Currently, most people on your team are having a hard time focusing because of too many emails, frequent instant messaging, and team members freely interrupting each other in their offices. You agree that you would all prefer to have fewer interruptions and distractions and to focus your mental energy in a more productive way; at the same time, you want to be able to access each other when you need support. In essence, you want to shift this norm:

- *FROM: Most of us are frequently interrupted and distracted by each other and multiple forms of technology so we are often frazzled and inefficient. This isn't something we talk about openly and no one seems to be able to do anything about it. It builds frustration and resentment and breeds inefficiency and overwhelm.*
- *TO: We have clear shared agreement on how we use emails, IMs, and in-person visits throughout the day and most of us honor those boundaries regularly. Most people report being able to carve out time for focused work on most days, while still being reasonably accessible to others.*

If your team is going to successfully change this norm, then most of the people on the team will need to change the way they *behave*. You and others might need to:

- Talk openly about this challenge and establish shared agreement on communication guidelines
- Put these guidelines in writing and post them in multiple places in the office so they are visible to everyone as a reminder
- Be mindful about who you include on emails and when you use "reply all" to reduce unnecessary emails
- Be mindful about how you choose to manage your own emails; perhaps setting new boundaries on closing your email app periodically, only checking it at certain times, etc.
- Be consistent about using the "busy" or "do not disturb" settings on your IM application so as to convey your status accurately
- Be consistent about *paying attention* to other people's IM status and honor their status by only chatting with them when they are available

These are just a few examples, but the point is this:

The only way a group norm changes is if the people in that group change their behaviors. If behaviors don't change, norms don't change. Individuals must change their own actions for the collective to evolve.

So, as we peel the onion back one more layer, we see that **changing culture requires changing how individuals *behave* in relation to each other.** (See Figure 2.4).

One More Step

While it's true that individual behaviors must evolve for culture to improve, our thinking can't stop at the level of behavior. This is because human beings usually only lastingly change our actions when we first evolve other internal aspects of ourselves such as:

- our in-the-moment thinking and long-term thought patterns
- our feelings and emotional processing practices, and
- our daily decisions and long-term decision-making models

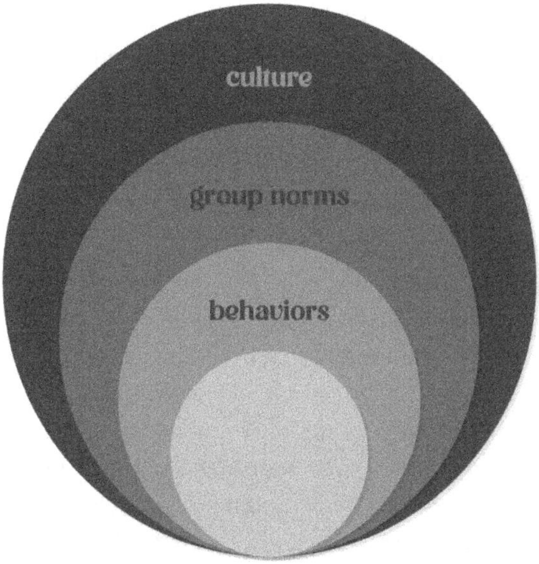

FIGURE 2.4 Concentric circles with behaviors.

In our work, we refer to these internal elements as our "inner operating systems."

The reality is that behaviors are always downstream consequences of our inner operating systems. One of the biggest reasons so many people who *really want to change* don't achieve their behavioral goals is because they don't understand, honor, or know how to operationalize this truth. Most people assume that the *desire and resolution to change* should be enough for them to improve or evolve in the way they want.

But that's not how humans work.

For example, let's say you want to change your behaviors around exercise. You *really want* to be exercising more because you know you'll feel better, sleep better, and look better. You've made a commitment to exercise three or four days a week, and you are C-O-M-M-I-T-T-E-D! You feel ready to finally make it happen.

You go to the gym consistently for a few months (or weeks or days), start to feel better about yourself . . . and then your motivation starts to wane, you notice yourself rationalizing why the gym isn't important today, and you go less and less often. Eventually, you find yourself right back where you started.

If this example doesn't resonate with you, replace it with any other example of a self-improvement goal you have committed to, but struggled to lastingly change.

If you have struggled to achieve your own behavioral improvements in any area, you may think your trouble is lack of willpower, motivation, time, or energy. In reality, the missing ingredient is that you overlooked the necessary *inner operating system update.*

Continuing with our exercise example, people who lastingly increase their activity level may have developed new inner narratives and self-talk about why exercise is important, what they "get" out of it, and why other things are less important. They have likely developed new ways of dealing with the common emotions of dread or resistance to exercise. And they very possibly (often without even knowing it) tapped into different personal values or motivators when deciding whether to prioritize exercise over other things. Their story that they don't have time for exercise is now a story about how exercise energizes and motivates them.

This same idea applies to culture work!

Humans Need Updates Too

Anyone who is going to significantly improve the way they behave *in relation to other people* will need an inner operating system update. They'll need to think differently about themselves and about other people, develop new practices for processing and regulating emotions, and tap into different mechanisms for making decisions.

Let's pause briefly on this idea of updating your inner operating system.

When something is updated—your phone, laptop, kitchen, or wardrobe—certain things are reduced or discarded because they no longer serve us well, and new things are added or enhanced that we didn't previously have the opportunity to use. In the case of technology, an update might remove bugs, glitches, and outdated software and introduce new software and applications. In the case of your kitchen, the update might include removing old countertops and appliances and introducing new fixtures and features.

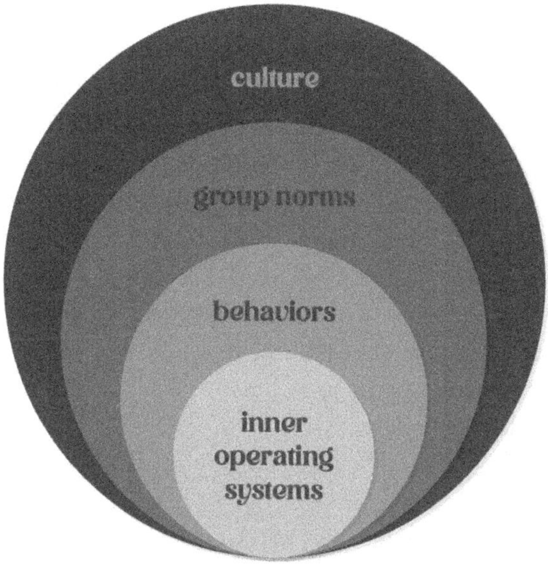

FIGURE 2.5 Concentric circles with iOS update.

The same thing is true for human updates. Updating our inner operating system requires important self-development work to discard outdated thinking patterns and habitual reactions, thereby creating space for more effective internal processes and more productive ways of relating with each other.

Ultimately, changing the culture of a work team or an entire organization requires that a group of people update their inner operating systems, at least a little bit, so they *relate more productively with each other*. (See Figure 2.5.)

To keep our language easy and relatable, we call this work of updating our iOS "Me Work."

Me Work

You'll hear a lot about "Me Work" in this book from this point forward.

Me Work is the personal work of updating our inner operating systems that individuals can *only do for themselves*. Me Work includes and results in an evolution in thinking, feeling, and decision-making that enables us to relate better with others and more effectively address the challenges and issues that inevitably arise. When a person is doing their Me Work, they become more effective in the world, often more satisfied with their lives, and more equipped to contribute to the development and nurturance of a thriving workplace culture.

While Me Work might take many forms, common examples include:

- Paying closer attention to our thinking and adjusting our internal narratives when they are undermining us
- Generating more empathy for others
- Not taking things personally
- Processing emotional discomfort in healthy ways so we don't project it onto others
- Reducing excessive connection to technology and/or work to create more balance
- Letting go of unhelpful anxiety, micromanaging, or the need to control

Me Work is such an important component of culture change, we dedicate the entire next chapter to it! The important things to know for now are:

- Me Work is about self-development and evolving thinking patterns, emotional processing, and decision-making
- Me Work is essential to culture change, and
- Me Work allows people to do their We Work, which is also essential for culture change

We Work

In terms of workplace culture, the most important result of consistent Me Work is that it enables powerful "We Work."

We Work is the interpersonal learning and growth that happens between two or more people in connection with each other. When done well, We Work results in healthier, more resilient relationships and greater collective effectiveness. In the workplace, it also results in a group's ability to navigate challenges and issues more effectively and to nurture their culture. (More on this in Chapter 5, "System Issues").

While We Work might also take many forms, common examples include:

- Purposefully incorporating moments of personal connection into our meetings and interactions
- Developing shared guidelines for meetings to ensure they are effective, and all voices are heard
- Asking more and better questions with each other to ensure our conversations get to the heart of what matters
- Practicing navigating difficult conversations directly, with a blend of truth and care (rather than avoiding them or becoming reactive or aggressive)

We Work is also essential to culture change, and we dedicate an entire chapter to this concept later in the book.

What you need to know for now is:

- We Work is about improving our interpersonal relationships, so they become healthier, stronger, and more connected
- People who do We Work together usually become more effective in the workplace and feel better about each other
- We Work happens best when the members of the group are actively doing their Me Work

What Me Work and We Work Have in Common

Ultimately, both Me Work (self-development) and We Work (improving relationships) are about the same thing: *a shift from reactivity to responsiveness.*

When we're relating with others in the workplace from the parts of our inner operating system that are outdated and unhelpful, we're more likely to be *reactive.* Reactivity develops as a result of many things including genetic predisposition, earlier life experiences, habit, ego, or simply mindlessness. As human beings, reactivity is our natural default state unless we consciously choose to operate differently. Even though it's our natural reactive state much of the time, it's not helpful because it results in behaviors such as:

- Interrupting other people to make a point
- Focusing on blame and who is wrong
- Taking things personally
- Making quick and inaccurate assumptions (and believing them without fact checking)
- Projecting our own uncomfortable emotions onto others
- Staying connected to work 24/7 unnecessarily and expecting others to do the same
- Trying to get power "over" people through manipulation or control

If left unchecked, this reactivity within and among us not only contributes to a mediocre or toxic culture, but also diminishes the team or organization's ability to commit and execute on important business essentials, such as:

- Establishing clarity and maintaining alignment
- Ideating and problem-solving collaboratively
- Resolving inevitable conflict productively
- Executing with quality
- And so on.

Conversely, when we're operating from a mindful *responsive* state, we are more likely to pay attention to the "now," stay open and curious, check our ego, and pause when we need to. When we're relating responsively, we're more likely to exhibit behaviors in relation to others that contribute to a thriving culture and drive important business results, such as:

- Listening with helpful intentions
- Asking powerful questions
- Talking directly to people instead of about them
- Maintaining perspective instead of taking things personally

- Evaluating our thoughts and assumptions for accuracy
- Regulating and processing our emotions in healthy ways so we don't project them onto others
- Taking personal responsibility for our intention, impact, and actions
- Striving to create "power with" by developing and elevating others

See Figure 2.6.

FIGURE 2.6 From reactive to responsive.

At the Heart of It

Ultimately, the work of culture transformation happens not when organizations make public statements about how important culture is or when they declare their company values. Those things are an important *starting point* for culture work, but they don't necessarily lead to any change in the way people behave.[3] Cultures also don't necessarily change for the better in response to investments in things like onsite fitness centers, ping-pong tables, or team-building events. That type of investment might be a sign that an organization has good intentions about improving the work experience for its people, but they are unlikely to sustainably change cultural norms in any significant way. True change happens only when many people in a group are *willing* and *able* to do their Me Work and We Work in an effort to move from reactivity to responsiveness.

Since Me Work and We Work are at the heart of culture change, we'll talk much more about these concepts in future chapters. For now, here's what you need to know:

- **Changing culture requires changing group norms.**
- **Changing group norms requires changing individual behaviors.**
- **Changing individual behaviors requires as many people as possible in the organization to actively do their Me and We Work.**

This Sounds Like Complex and Time-Consuming Work!

If you are thinking this, you are right!

Changing culture is complex because human beings are complex. And changing culture takes time because human beings usually make significant changes gradually over time. But when it happens, it's incredibly rewarding. Just like investing in our families or ourselves, improving culture can feel daunting but, when we do it with the right mindset, skills, and support, we have a chance to discover a whole new way of being. The outcome is worth the effort.

3 Me Work

Paul

Paul is a newly promoted manager in a county government organization. As part of an investment in workplace culture, the county administrator has requested that all new managers work with a professional coach during their first year.

In our second coaching session, Paul and I (Rebecca) are talking about how his avoidance of conflict—or anything that feels like conflict—has become very problematic for him. He's aware that he rarely speaks truthfully with other people when he thinks it might make them uncomfortable. When he has difficult feedback to share with a member of his team, he procrastinates so issues often escalate unnecessarily. And if things get even remotely heated in a conversation, he shuts down, "caves in," or changes the subject just to end the conversation.

Paul shares a recent example with me. One of his team members had missed an important deadline and he knew he needed to be direct about the impact. Instead, he sugarcoated the conversation until it barely felt like feedback at all. He was pretty sure his team member walked away thinking it wasn't a big deal, while Paul's worry continued to simmer beneath the surface.

As Paul is describing this tendency, I ask him what it feels like when he imagines giving tough feedback or has to navigate a tense conversation. "My stomach twists up," he says. "I'm so worried that they'll be offended by something I say or view me as cold or no longer 'one of them.'"

His tendency to avoid or sugarcoat has already been problematic in his personal relationships, especially with his wife. At home, he often feels like his own needs and wants aren't prioritized (because he doesn't communicate them clearly) and then he feels resentful. He wants to get out of this pattern with his wife but isn't sure how to fix this situation at home either.

Now that Paul has recently been promoted to a leadership position with direct reports and a higher level of accountability, he's feeling more pressure to get better. He has worked for bosses in the past who avoid directness and conflict, and he knows the damage that can do to a team. Without the ability to speak candidly and navigate friction, he won't be able to lead his team well.

By the end of the coaching session, Paul has more clarity about why he avoids candor and conflict. It's important to him that other people perceive him as a nice person. He's worried about offending others or hurting their feelings. And he doesn't know what to do when other people get uncomfortable or mad.

I express appreciation to Paul for both his commitment to doing this work and his awareness about *why* he has developed this counterproductive style of communication. I ask him:

> "What needs to happen internally for you to become more skilled and confident with speaking candidly and navigating friction?"

Paul is silent for a minute and then talks at length as he processes out loud the possible answers. In summary, he shares:

- I'm going to have to figure out how to be okay with the fact that other people might be upset with me or a decision I've made
- I have to stop worrying so much about being "nice"—or at least redefine what it means to be a nice person
- I have to learn how to handle my own discomfort and other people's emotions when they run high

Paul is spot on—and he's just identified some of his Me Work.

If Paul invests time and energy into doing his Me Work, he'll not only become a more effective communicator; he'll be making an important contribution to improving his team's workplace culture.

It Starts with You

Spoiler alert! The point we want to make in this chapter is this:

You—yes, YOU—have influence on your workplace culture, no matter what your role or title is or where you sit in the organization. One way you start to influence your culture is by focusing on the things you have direct control over. As much as we might like to believe we have control over lots of people and circumstances, the reality is that each of us only has control over ourselves: our actions and reactions, which are fueled by our inner operating system.

You know now that Me Work and We Work are essential to successful improvements in a group's culture. People who are self-aware, open to practicing new ways of being, and are intentional about the way they relate with other people—in other words, people who do their Me Work—are at the heart of a thriving culture.

Me Work is crucial not just in designing and nurturing an intentional culture; it's essential for living to our full potential. We often hear from our clients that this work has been unexpectedly beneficial to them personally and in relationships outside of work too.

The first person I remember sharing this with us was Alison, a participant in an early training with one of our government clients. At the start of the third or fourth training session, she said:

> "You know, my husband loves that I'm taking this training! It's actually improving my marriage. I'm applying what we're learning to my home life and I notice a difference."

Alison was right when she described the bonus that engaging in meaningful culture work includes for those who really show up for it: *What we learn about ourselves and others in the context of work is directly applicable to our lives outside of work*. When we do our Me Work, we become better people and we *relate* with others better: our children, our siblings, our parents, our friends, our neighbors—and definitely our colleagues.

In the rest of this chapter, we'll explore Me Work in depth. We'll identify common examples of Me Work and learn about our many options for engaging in Me Work. By the end of this chapter, you'll have identified at least one form of Me Work that will change the way you behave in a way that directly impacts the culture on your team.

The Three Types of Me Work: Energy, Connection, and Courage

Human nature is complicated, and we should be cautious about oversimplifying. But our brains learn best when new ideas are presented in simple frameworks that are easy to understand and retain. Our experience has taught us that Me Work (and We Work) can be understood through the lens of these three categories: energy, connection, and courage.

Energy Me Work

Energy Me Work is about developing greater awareness, language, skills, and practices that help us elevate, replenish, and direct our physical, mental, emotional, and spiritual energy.[1] It empowers us to feel more energized and relate with others more effectively.

Even though energy is our primary fuel for life, most of us learn very little about it in childhood or adolescence. While our formal education teaches us a lot about math, science, reading, and writing, we don't typically learn about *ourselves and our energy*. Many adults enter the workplace ill-equipped to understand and manage their own energy well.

When we do our Energy Me Work well, we often find that we're able to make gradual and important shifts in ourselves—*even while navigating the same complexities of the workplace*:

From	To
High or chronic stress without adequate coping mechanisms	Reduced stress and greater ability to navigate and harness stress to create resilience
Negatively impacted physical health	Better physical health and fitness
Uncomfortable or unpleasant emotions	More comfortable or pleasant emotions
Lack of skill in navigating our emotions	Greater self-awareness, skill, and confidence in navigating our emotions and responding to other people's emotions
Mental multi-tasking and frazzle	Mental focus and clarity
Lack of presence	Greater presence
Less or low-quality energy	More and higher-quality energy
Going through the motions without meaning	A clear sense of purpose that directs our energy investments

Connection Me Work

Connection Me Work is about prioritizing strong interpersonal relationships over ego, defensiveness, or being right. Connection Me Work is about taking responsibility for our inner operating system so that we become more open and available to give the best of ourselves to others—and receive the best others have to offer with both grace and healthy boundaries. When we do our Connection Me Work well, we end up seeing the reality of others more clearly and communicating with more truth and care.

One of the biggest reasons Connection Me Work is so important is because humans are hard-wired to need and seek connection with others. To live and work to our potential, we need to feel like we belong and are accepted and valued for who we really are. On one hand, this is a good set up for business because most significant organizational achievements result not from a single individual but from the connection and collaboration between multiple individuals. Ironically, despite our innate need for connection, our default reactivity often leads to behaviors that *disconnect* us from other people. We often mindlessly choose being right or maintaining a self-image, usually to the demise of genuine connection with others.

When we do our Connection Me Work, we tend to notice subtle and sometimes overt differences in the way we feel and relate—*even with people who do not seem to be doing their own Me Work*. Over time, we are gradually able to shift:

From	To
Emotionally closed off or unavailable to others	More open and emotionally available for others
Unreceptive to or dismissive of new ideas and different perspectives	Able and willing to consider other ideas and navigate different perspectives
Ineffective communication	Communicating clearly, directly, and kindly
Anxious around, upset with, or disappointed in others	Experiencing ease, compassion, joy, and grace in our relationships with others
Quick to make wrong assumptions or unnecessarily critical judgments about others	Staying in curiosity longer and seeing reality more clearly
Too self-focused or co-dependent	Balanced in our focus on self and others

Courage Me Work

Courage Me Work is about strengthening our integrity muscles so that we do what is right or necessary more often, even when it feels hard or risky. Courage Me Work helps us clarify our values and act in accordance even when it means we need to walk through fear or discomfort in order to do so.

Courage Me Work doesn't mean we *stop* feeling afraid or vulnerable; it means we get more comfortable experiencing those feelings and following our internal North Star anyway. Over time, Courage Me Work reduces the amount of fear or anxiety we experience because we learn that choosing courage in the face of vulnerability breeds connection, builds resilience, and elevates energy more often than it results in negative consequences. We also learn that, even when negative consequences from brave choices arise, we can handle them.

Courage Me Work often results in important shifts:

From	To
Uncertainty about how to behave or doing what we think others want us to do (instead of what we know is right)	Greater confidence and conviction in our choices even if others might disagree or disapprove
Defaulting to what is easy or comfortable even if it's out of alignment with our values	Choosing what is hard or uncomfortable to be in alignment with our values
Contributing to, supporting, or enabling unethical choices or activities	Removing ourselves from unethical circumstances or speaking up against unethical or immoral activities
Avoiding or sugar-coating hard conversations	Speaking directly and truthfully with care
Avoiding conflict or acting defensively in conflict situations	Navigating conflict mindfully with minimal defensiveness
Lacking sincerity or being unreliable	Holding ourselves accountable to sincerity and reliability
Perfectionism	Healthy striving

Everyone Has Me Work to Do

The bad news is that we all have Me Work to do. And the good news is that we all have Me Work to do! All of us at least occasionally fall into default states of reactivity or mindlessness and show up for others in a less-than-ideal way. No matter our age, title, race, socioeconomic status, gender, or anything else—we each have opportunities for self-improvement.

The difference between people is not whether they *have* Me Work to do; the difference is whether they *choose* to do it. Those of us who want to live and work to our potential and contribute to the strength and effectiveness of the groups we are a part of; we choose to do it. If you are interested in improving the culture on your team or in your family (or anywhere else), the work starts with YOU.

What's Your Me Work?

Now is your opportunity to find out.

Over the next few pages, we'll share many examples of Me Work that fall into the three categories of energy, connection, and courage. You'll notice there are bigger examples of Me Work with specific examples under each.

As you read the list below, put an "X" or a checkmark in any box that describes Me Work that would be helpful to you. If you think improving in this way might make you show up for yourself and others better and contribute more effectively at work, give it a mark. If you have other ideas for Me Work that aren't here, put them in the "other" lines.

You might mark lots of boxes or only a few. You might find that a lot of your possible Me Work falls more heavily into one category, or you might find your opportunities are spread out across all three categories. There are no right or wrong answers here. This is just about awareness.

What's Your Energy Me Work?

- ☐ ***Physical energy (sleep):*** **Prioritize sleep and rest so I have high-quality energy for the people and things that matter most.**
  - ☐ Commit to turning off screens by a certain time to go to bed earlier
  - ☐ Remove technology and blue light from my bedroom
  - ☐ Minimize caffeine later in the day
  - ☐ Minimize alcohol later in the day
  - ☐ Establish and commit to more consistent sleep times
  - ☐ Establish bedtime rituals that can be practiced anywhere (home, travel, vacation, etc.)
  - ☐ Practice deep breathing or other mindfulness strategies before falling asleep or getting back to sleep
  - ☐ Other: ______________________________
- ☐ ***Physical energy (movement):*** **Prioritize movement during the workday so I have high-quality energy and**

physical stamina for the people and things that matter most.

- ☐ Alternate between sitting and standing throughout the day
- ☐ Incorporate more micro-movements into my daily life (i.e., stairs instead of elevators, stretching, walking to see people instead of calling or messaging, walking meetings)
- ☐ Other: ______________________________

☐ ***Physical energy (exercise):*** **Prioritize high-intensity, uncomfortable (not painful) exercise to increase my energy capacity and counteract the aging process.**

- ☐ Increase high-intensity cardiorespiratory exercise each week[2] (i.e., fast walking, HIIT swimming, pickleball)
- ☐ Increase the amount of high-intensity strength training (body weight exercises, resistance machines, free weights, Pilates, yoga)
- ☐ Stretch regularly
- ☐ Other: ______________________________

☐ ***Physical energy (fuel):*** **Eat more mindfully so my body has the right type and amount of food to be at its best.**

- ☐ Eat to the point of "satisfied" rather than "full" or "overfull"
- ☐ When I want high-quality energy for the next few hours, choose types and amounts of food that will provide that type of energy instead of foods that will make me tired or lethargic
- ☐ Learn to notice the difference between physiological hunger and non-hunger triggers for eating (time, stress, boredom, seeing food)
- ☐ Practice using hunger as my guide for eating and attending to non-hunger triggers in more productive ways
- ☐ Other: ______________________________

☐ ***Mental energy:* Enact and honor better boundaries around technology to reduce distractions and increase mental focus**

- ☐ Turn my phone off or put it out of sight when I need mental focus or want to be present with others
- ☐ Carve out and protect time each day or several times each week for uninterrupted work
- ☐ Establish and honor guidelines for myself on checking and responding to email
- ☐ Learn about and use the focus tools my technology already has to benefit me (i.e., "focus mode," "do not disturb," etc.)
- ☐ Improve the way I prioritize my work responsibilities (to-do lists, apps, etc.)
- ☐ Other: ________________________________

☐ ***Mental energy:* Improve my ability to be more in charge of my own thinking and storytelling when it is creating stress or mental distraction**

- ☐ Practice techniques such as thought stopping or cognitive reframing to interrupt or change my thinking patterns when I need to
- ☐ Practice techniques such as mindfulness meditation to be able to quiet thinking and establish calm and presence
- ☐ Check my assumptions (notice when I'm making up a story without all the facts)
- ☐ Other: ________________________________

☐ ***Emotional energy:* Become more equipped to understand and navigate my own emotions productively so I don't use unhealthy coping skills or discharge negativity onto other people**

- ☐ With a therapist, coach, trusted friend, or even while alone journaling, explore and attend to unprocessed trauma, unhelpful personality tendencies, or life experiences that generate recurring negative emotions for me

- ☐ Become more aware of when I'm emotionally triggered and practice processing skills to return to a calm, centered state reasonably soon
- ☐ Intentionally practice emotional micro recovery strategies about every 60–90 minutes to create emotional awareness and regulation (going for a walk outside, stretching, deep breathing, gratitude, journaling, music, etc.)
- ☐ When I notice I've become emotionally reactive, pause and practice a helpful strategy
- ☐ Other: ____________________

☐ ***Emotional energy:* Develop more emotional intelligence by increasing my skills and confidence in understanding and navigating other people's emotions**

- ☐ Increase my emotional literacy: Take a course, read a book, or learn in another way about the broad spectrum of human emotions
- ☐ Practice talking openly with other people about their emotional experiences with the aim to learn
- ☐ Practice active observation by paying attention to more than words when others are talking (i.e., body language, tone, facial expression)
- ☐ Build a habit of pausing before responding, especially when I feel emotionally triggered in response to another's words or actions
- ☐ Other: ____________________

☐ ***All energy:* Reduce excessive connection to work so that I can avoid the detrimental effects of overworking and prioritize other important elements of my life**

- ☐ Explore the reasons I work so much and address the underlying causes
- ☐ Develop the skill and confidence to have a direct conversation with my boss or team about boundaries at work

- ☐ Create and honor boundaries that protect my energy so I don't show up exhausted for the people and things that matter most
- ☐ Other: ___________________________________

☐ ***All energy:* Align my energy investments with what's most important to me**

- ☐ Complete the "Aligning My Energy Investments" exercise on our website
- ☐ Discuss with a therapist, coach, partner, or trusted friend how I'm currently aligning energy versus how I want to be
- ☐ Choose *one* area of energy management to improve and focus on that improvement now
- ☐ Other: ___________________________________

What's Your Connection Me Work?

While there are many examples of Connection Me Work, here are some that arise frequently in our work with clients and in our own personal experiences. Again, check boxes that resonate with you and add your "others" in the blank lines.

☐ **Improve my mindset and thinking patterns**

- ☐ Shift unhelpful or limiting thought patterns about other people
- ☐ Notice when I am stuck in judgmental thinking about another person and shift my narrative
- ☐ Pay attention to negative self-talk and replace it with a more supportive inner voice
- ☐ Identify my default stories about people or situations and practice considering alternative perspectives
- ☐ Practice giving others the benefit of the doubt rather than assuming negative intent
- ☐ Reframe challenges as opportunities to learn and grow
- ☐ Practice gratitude by noticing and naming what is going well each day

- ☐ Catch myself in "all-or-nothing" or perfectionistic thinking and practice a more balanced perspective
- ☐ Notice when I am focused on problems and redirect my thinking toward possible solutions
- ☐ Other: ______________________________

☐ **Improve my communication skills (general)**

- ☐ Increase my self-awareness about my strengths and gaps with communication
- ☐ Learn about and practice empathy[3] more often
- ☐ Practice listening more intentionally to others (with the intention to learn or understand, rather than to reply)
- ☐ Watch for impulses to interrupt; practice waiting for the other person to finish
- ☐ Focus on asking helpful questions and "telling" less often
- ☐ Practice being more succinct and getting to the point more quickly
- ☐ Pay attention to my tone of voice and ensure it conveys care
- ☐ Pay attention to my body language and ensure it conveys openness

☐ **Improve my ability to communicate with more candor**

- ☐ Learn about the importance of candor
- ☐ Identify my concerns about speaking directly and begin to address them
- ☐ Practice revealing more and withholding[4] less, at first with people who feel "safe" to practice with
- ☐ Practice giving difficult feedback more directly
- ☐ Observe what happens when I speak truthfully and reflect on lessons
- ☐ Other: ______________________________

☐ **Reduce my tendency for reactivity and defensiveness**

- ☐ Define how less reactivity and defensiveness will improve my life and relationships
- ☐ Identify my physical and emotional signs of defensiveness (heart racing, tense muscles, impulse to shut down)

- ☐ Notice when I am taking things personally and practice doing so less often
- ☐ Identify what I can do when I start to get defensive to stay calm and receptive (breathe deeply, focus on listening, repeat a mantra to myself, relax my body)
- ☐ When I start to feel myself getting defensive, practice my identified strategies and notice what happens in the conversation
- ☐ Learn what underlying mechanisms lead to defensiveness and address those (a strong need to be right, taking things too personally too often, etc.)
- ☐ Other:________________________________

☐ **Increase my ability to demonstrate genuine care for others**

- ☐ Ensure my tone of voice demonstrates care rather than irritation, disinterest, or condescension
- ☐ Learn people's names, how to pronounce them, and how to spell them
- ☐ Learn what's important to people and remember it
- ☐ Start more of my work interactions with personal connection first
- ☐ Practice self-compassion[5] so that I can demonstrate compassion for others

☐ **Increase my ability to demonstrate sincerity for others**

- ☐ Notice when I am concealing information to protect myself or the other person's feelings
- ☐ Say what I mean, clearly, as often as I can
- ☐ Keep my messages consistent from person to person
- ☐ Make sure my actions align with my words

☐ **Improve my reliability**

- ☐ Be honest with myself about what I can and can't do so that I don't overcommit and then appear unreliable when I can't deliver on time

- ☐ Practice boundaries and saying "no" when necessary
- ☐ When I do agree to take something on, do what I say I am going to do—or be honest with the other person if I cannot
- ☐ Other: ______________________________

☐ **Respond to mistakes more effectively (mine and others)**

- ☐ Practice acceptance about the fact that human beings are fallible and we all make mistakes; no one is perfect
- ☐ When I make a mistake, admit it to myself and openly to others
- ☐ View my own mistakes as opportunities for learning and a pathway for growth
- ☐ Practice reducing shame or harsh judgment directed at myself (self-compassion)
- ☐ When others make a mistake, view it as an opportunity for learning rather than judgment
- ☐ Discuss mistakes with others with a sense of curiosity and an aim to learn or improve
- ☐ Get better at asking for help so I make fewer avoidable mistakes
- ☐ Other: ______________________________

☐ **Improve my ability to navigate friction and conflict productively**

- ☐ Learn to differentiate between unhealthy conflict (arguing to win or disrespectful language) versus healthy friction (different ideas being presented for consideration in a meeting or addressing an unresolved issue)
- ☐ Explore my personal beliefs around conflict and identify those that don't serve me well ("All conflict is bad and means something is wrong" or "It's important that I'm right or that I win")
- ☐ Practice internal strategies for keeping myself calm and centered when friction arises

- ☐ Learn language that can help me navigate conflict ("rumble" language, powerful questions, or sentence starters)
- ☐ Identify one situation where conflict regularly arises and establish a plan for handling it differently
- ☐ Other: ____________________

☐ **Reduce my attachment to the need for control**

- ☐ Examine how my need for control saps my energy or disconnects me from other people
- ☐ Explore where the need to control comes from and begin to address root cause issues
- ☐ Practice new narratives and self-talk that can help me "let go" when I need to ("This is not a situation I need to control right now" or "It will be okay if I let go a little bit" or "This person is capable and if a mistake is made, we can handle it")
- ☐ Use the concept of the Sphere of Control to redirect my energy toward what I can control (more on this in Chapter 5)
- ☐ Other: ____________________

What's Your Courage Me Work?

☐ **Use a values-based decision-making model to help me navigate situations that require courage**

- ☐ Identify my non-negotiable personal values
- ☐ Consider vulnerable situations through the lens of values and make decisions that keep me in alignment with my non-negotiable values
- ☐ When I am tempted to choose something that is not congruent with my values because it feels easier or safer, explore my reasons for doing so in writing or out loud with another person
- ☐ Practice making the choice that is in alignment with my values more often; reflect on my experiences and lessons learned
- ☐ Other: ____________________

- ☐ **Reduce my concern about other people's approval to free up energy for making courageous choices**
  - ☐ Identify how my need to be liked or approved of sometimes leads to making choices that are easy or fast rather than right
  - ☐ Explore where my need for approval comes from in writing or out loud with another person
  - ☐ Play the "worst case scenario" game: *If I make the courageous choice and so-and-so disapproves, what is the worst that will happen? Am I willing to risk that?*
  - ☐ Other: ______________________________
- ☐ **Become more courageous specifically in the areas of diversity, equity, inclusion, and belonging**
  - ☐ Through courses, podcasts, books, or conversations, learn about these concepts more fully: what they mean and why they are important for everyone
  - ☐ Explore how my own identity (gender, race, socioeconomic status, life experiences, etc.) create advantages or disadvantages for me and practice openly discussing that with other people
  - ☐ Learn about the concept of unconscious bias and begin to notice how my own bias affects my narratives and actions toward others
  - ☐ Learn about the concept of allyship[6] and identify where I might act as an ally for others; then choose one or more acts of allyship and practice them
  - ☐ Other: ______________________________
- ☐ **Speak up about systems or structures that are not serving people well**
  - ☐ Identify situations where silence or dysfunction has allowed harmful or unhelpful systems or norms to persist
  - ☐ Practice respectfully raising concerns with decision-makers, even when it feels risky

- ☐ Gather allies or data to strengthen my voice, but do not wait for "perfect conditions" before speaking up
- ☐ Reflect on what happens when I do speak truthfully about system-level issues and adjust my approach over time
- ☐ Other: ______________________________

☐ **Challenge the status quo when it limits growth, innovation, or fairness**

- ☐ Reflect on how challenging the status quo creates progress—for myself, my team, or the broader organization
- ☐ Notice when "we've always done it this way" is used as a reason for maintaining a process, policy, or tradition and consider calling attention to this default perspective
- ☐ Ask bold questions that surface whether the current way is truly the best way
- ☐ Practice offering alternatives or experiments rather than only pointing out problems
- ☐ Other: ______________________________

☐ **Take risks in service of long-term impact rather than short-term comfort**

- ☐ Notice when fear of failure, criticism, or discomfort leads me to choose the "safe" path
- ☐ Define what long-term impact looks like in my role or organization and align my choices with that bigger picture
- ☐ Practice experimenting with small, calculated risks and reflect on the results
- ☐ Identify leaders or peers who have modeled courageous risk-taking and learn from their examples
- ☐ Other: ______________________________

How to Think About Your Me Work

How are you feeling now that you've identified your Me Work? Maybe you found this exercise energizing because it helped you identify what you can take charge of and where to start. Maybe you're feeling overwhelmed at the thought of all the work you might need to do. Maybe you're somewhere in between. However you're feeling, there are a few important things to keep in mind:

1. Progress, not perfection. This cliché is overused but essential here. Improving workplace culture doesn't require human beings to be perfect, which is a relief because perfection is not possible. Culture work simply asks us to do better for ourselves and each other *more of the time*.
2. Evolving ourselves so we can more positively impact the cultures we are a part of takes time, energy, and dedication. Since we only have so much of each, we need to be realistic about our Me Work endeavors. Most people can only change themselves in one or two significant ways at a time. If you checked a lot of boxes on the Me Work lists, consider narrowing down your Me Work to no more than two development opportunities you can act on in the short term. You could choose development opportunities that you feel more confident about so you can make progress quickly and experience an energizing win; or you might choose to attend to a development opportunity that is harder but will have a more substantial impact on your culture.
3. Me Work often requires engaging in practices that deepen self-awareness, expand our perspective, change internal narratives, shift the way we respond to emotions, and allow us to test new ways of being. While you can expect a few big "a-ha!" moments that result in immediate and lasting changes in behaviors, you should also expect your Me Work to be two-steps-forward and one-step-back. Setbacks are a part of the process and to be expected.
4. If you are still wondering why this book on workplace culture takes such a deep dive into Me Work, remember this important connection: workplace culture is the result of collective group norms. Norms are the result of individual behaviors interacting with each other. Behaviors are the result of inner operating systems. If your workplace culture is going to improve, the people in that group—including you—will need to evolve your inner operating systems so that you show up more effectively for each other. Collective change depends on individual change. Since the only individual you have control over is you, your Me Work is the best place to start.
5. One bonus benefit of Me Work is that even if you leave your current workplace culture or give up trying to change it, your Me Work still benefits you. You get to take it with you no matter where you go.

Is It a Technical Problem or an Adaptive Challenge?

As you are considering your Me Work, it's also important to know that self-development ranges on a spectrum from relatively simple and "easy" to very complex and very difficult. One way to think about this is through the lens of "adaptive challenges" versus "technical challenges." These terms were originally introduced by Ronald Heifetz in his 1994 book *Leadership Without Easy Answers.*[7] Heifetz and his colleague Marty Linsky later elaborated on these concepts and described the need to differentiate and respond differently:

- Technical challenges usually involve one or more problems that are fairly easy to identify. Both the problem and its solution are recognizable based on past experience. Technical challenges often feel simpler and have a quicker "fix" we can implement based on other people's expertise.
- Adaptive challenges are complex problems that can only be effectively addressed or resolved with changes in people's values, beliefs, and loyalties. They are often less understood and require more learning and adaptation by those involved. Adaptive challenges cannot usually be addressed by technical expertise alone; they require that people make internal changes or, in our language, update their inner operating systems significantly.

While Heifetz and Linsky introduced this idea originally focusing on organizational challenges, the idea can be applied to individuals as well. Let's learn about Alexa's journey with Me Work to understand the difference between adaptive challenges and technical problems when it comes to personal self-development.

Alexa

Alexa is the Vice President of Product Development in a technology firm that hired us to help develop their leaders so they can most effectively influence culture and organizational performance.

Alexa works long hours, struggles to spend enough time with her husband and young children, and feels she is teetering on the brink of burnout. The results of a recent employee engagement survey indicated that her department scored lower on several important cultural metrics than other departments. In a recent 360, she received feedback that many of her team members feel unable to grow professionally and contribute fully because she does not provide the autonomy they are capable of handling. They are feeling micro-managed and frustrated because Alexa is often the hold-up for projects getting completed.

Alexa has enlisted the support of one of our professional coaches to work on this. In her first session, she says she knows she needs to get better at delegating and not doing it all herself.

> "It's so frustrating to me that I can't get better at this. I've read a lot about delegation and even went to a workshop a few months ago. I could recite the steps of good delegation by memory. Why am I so stuck?"

This is a perfect example of a personal adaptive challenge at work.

It's not that Alexa lacks knowledge about the importance of delegation or *how* to delegate. In theory, she knows the solution. But knowledge in this case is a technical fix—straightforward skills and processes she could learn. And Alexa's challenge is not a technical problem.

It's an adaptive challenge rooted deeper within her need for control, her reluctance to trust others fully, and the quiet fear that if she lets go, her value as a leader would shrink. This isn't a matter of a better task tracker or clearer instructions. It's an adaptive challenge that will require her to shift her mindset, confront her own insecurities, and redefine what it means to succeed as a leader.

Like Alexa, most of us have at least a few personal adaptive challenges that our Me Work will need to address.

As you look back over the list of Me Work, which iOS updates might be technical problems that can be solved with expertise and quick behavior changes? And which might be more complex adaptive challenges that are going to require significant shifts *within* you?

One way you can differentiate adaptive challenges from technical problems is to pay attention to your body and your mind as you consider each form of potential Me Work you identified. You'll know you're looking at an adaptive challenge if your stomach flips or you experience some other surge of anxiety at the thought of actually making the change. Adaptive challenges by their very nature require us to step into discomfort and leave behind the familiar and comfortable. While adaptive Me Work is harder and usually takes more time, it's also the place where we have the greatest opportunity to fulfill our potential and impact culture.

How to Do Your Me Work

Our experience has taught us that Me Work is usually best done with a multifaceted approach. Sometimes we can do our Me Work on our own through reflection, journaling, and personal practices that don't involve other people. More often, Me Work requires support from or interaction with others.

Here is a list of avenues for doing your Me Work.

Take a formal course:
A structured class can give you both the knowledge and the step-by-step framework to build new skills or shift your mindset. For example, if you want to improve your ability to manage stress so you're not so reactive with others, you might take a course on mindfulness and then practice the techniques you learn throughout the day. You can find a variety of courses on our website. (See the callout box at the end of this chapter for the URL.)

Read:
Books, articles, and research can open your mind to fresh perspectives and give you practical tools for growth. For instance, if you want to become less judgmental and more inclusive, you might read a book that helps you understand the concept of unconscious bias, assess your own, and learn how to be more aware of or override your default bias settings. You can find a list of our favorite books that relate to Me Work on our website. (See the callout box at the end of this chapter for the URL.)

Listen:
Podcasts, audiobooks, and recorded talks make it easy to learn from others' experiences and expertise even while you're doing other things. If you want to elevate your ability to inspire cultural change on your team, you

might find a compelling leadership or culture podcast, listen periodically, jot down key takeaways, and experiment with new ideas as you relate with members of your team. You can find a list of our favorite Me Work podcasts, including our podcast *Energy, Connection and Courage* on our website. (See the callout box at the end of this chapter for the URL.)

Talk with others:
Honest, open conversations can help you see blind spots, learn from others' experiences, and feel less alone in your journey. For instance, if you are struggling with excessive interruptions and distractions at work and having trouble focusing, consider talking with other colleagues about your frustration and desire for a different working experience. This might result in you learning how other people are handling the same challenge or even joining forces with other colleagues to create systemic change on your team (which would be an example of Me Work resulting in We Work—but more on that in the next chapter).

Journal:
Writing down your thoughts, feelings, and observations helps you process experiences and clarify purpose, progress, inspiration, and lessons learned. For example, if you want to get better at navigating conflict, you might journal first about your conflict stories to identify how your current thinking is or is not serving you well. That same journal might serve as the place you keep inspiring thoughts and reflect on the lessons you are learning as you practice approaching conflict situations differently.

Work with a professional coach:
Working with a skilled coach is one of the best methods of making quick and substantial progress with your Me Work. Regular sessions with a coach can help you laser in on root cause issues, challenge your own thinking, and explore new ideas and ways of being. In Alexa's case, working with a professional coach was the most important commitment for increasing her ability to delegate, which freed up her ability to focus on high-impact work and reduce frustration on her team. For more on how to find a coach, visit our website. (See the callout box at the end of this chapter for the URL.)

Work with a therapist:
While there is some overlap between coaching and therapy, these are two distinct avenues for Me Work. If you work with a quality therapist, therapy

provides a safe space to explore deeper emotional patterns, heal past experiences, and build resilience. For example, a therapist could help you unpack recurring trust issues so you can address opening yourself up to others more often. For a checklist to use in finding the best therapist, visit our website.

Join a group:
Being part of a group of people who share similar challenges and want similar changes can provide encouragement, perspective, and a sense of belonging. For example, if you are struggling with compulsive over-connection to technology, you might join a support group for people who are reducing dependence on technology. Or, if you want to exercise more regularly to increase your physical stamina, you might join a rec group with people who meet regularly to be active in a way you like.

Create accountability mechanisms for yourself:
In his book *Atomic Habits,*[8] author James Clear suggests that "We don't rise to the level of our individual goals; we fall to the level of our systems." Most of us need accountability systems in place to help support our personal efforts at change. Many of the avenues listed already serve as accountability support, including working with a coach or therapist or joining a group. Outside of those, you might consider making verbal commitments to people who are important to you and asking them to check in with you periodically on how these commitments are coming along—or using technology wisely for reminders, scheduling, and automated support.

Complimentary resources available at: www.vidlwork.com/culturejourneybook

- Reflection tool: Aligning My Energy Investments
- List of Powerful Questions
- "Rumble Language" from Brene Brown
- Reflection tool: Sphere of Control
- List of our favorite books, many of which support Me Work
- List of our favorite podcasts, many of which support Me Work

4 We Work

"We Talk in Circles"

I (Rebecca) am leading a facilitated conversation for a leadership team at a university. Today, we are focusing on the group's difficulty in resolving issues effectively. We've been working with this team for several months, so they have improved their communication skills with each other and are more comfortable speaking candidly.

To start, I ask the group to describe what typically happens as they try to resolve issues together. There is a long pause. Eventually, Jennifer, a Vice President, speaks:

> "I feel like we talk in circles but never actually decide anything. Or we decide a few things but there's no follow through or accountability. It seems like we spend a lot of time talking about issues, but we don't get anywhere. The rest of the college suffers because we take a long time to make important decisions and change issues that are impacting our people."

I thank Jennifer for going first and speaking honestly and then ask the group:

> Would someone be willing to share what this experience is like for you?

There is another long pause. I hear Terry sigh deeply and I invite him to share what his sigh means.

> "I wouldn't have said this a few months ago, but I feel like I can go out on a limb and say this now. Honestly, our conversations about issues drive me nuts. I'm even noticing I'm starting to feel resentful about coming to these meetings."

Others in the room nod their heads and some laugh uncomfortably.

I wasn't surprised to hear this because I had heard similar sentiments from other people on the leadership team. We had heard in coaching sessions that one leader had a tendency to repeat himself, another often diverted the conversation with unhelpful tangents, the team's leader struggled to manage these dynamics effectively. By the time this facilitated conversation happened, it had become clear that there were accidental, unhelpful norms that had developed among the members of this leadership team that were undermining the team's ability to resolve issues and eroding leaders' relationships with each other.

I ask the group: "What do you think needs to happen on the team in order for you to more productively resolve issues?"

Emboldened by the verbal support from Terry, Jennifer chimes in again:

> "I don't know exactly but I feel like someone in the group needs to take charge of the conversations because we need to make sure we stay on track and get to resolution. I think we could benefit from shared agreement on guidelines that help us keep meetings effective. It's like we're all working with different understandings—or no understanding at all—about what we're supposed to be doing in these meetings. I think some of us need to get a little bolder about acknowledging when the conversation has become ineffective instead of waiting for someone else to say it, which never happens. We all just seem to tolerate it and then complain about it after the meeting is over."

In her response, Jennifer is describing an example of We Work.

If Jennifer and her team invest time and energy into doing what she suggests, they will not only have more effective meetings and resolve issues more quickly, but they will also take a big step toward improving the culture of their leadership team and, eventually, the entire organization.

What Is We Work?

The simplest definition of We Work is:

> **Two or more people intentionally learning and growing together for the sake of strengthening the relationship and improving the group's functioning.**

Here are two things to know about We Work:

- We Work almost always involves *talking* with each other in new ways or about things that have previously not been said. **Candor and courage are essential elements of We Work.**
- For people to successfully do their We Work, they usually have to be doing Me Work that supports the relational change.

In the rest of this chapter, we'll explore We Work more fully. As we did with Me Work, we'll identify common examples of We Work and you'll learn how you might do We Work with one other person, a few, or your entire team. By the end of this chapter, you'll have identified at least one form of We Work you think your work team might need to do—and you'll know how you can be a catalyst for that work, or at least a champion of it.

Energy, Connection, and Courage

While Me Work falls a bit more neatly into the categories of energy, connection, and courage, We Work does not. That's because We Work usually requires and results in more of *all three*. So rather than describe examples of We Work through those three categories, we'll describe how each of these three ideas relates to We Work.

Energy

When we do our We Work well together, important energy shifts happen both *within* each person and *among* the members of the group.

When a relationship or a group of people need We Work but haven't done it, the people in the group are often energetically burdened or undermined. Think about the last time you experienced drama, dysfunction, or less-than-ideal performance on your team. How did that affect your personal energy and well-being? Maybe you experienced frequent or chronic stress or tension that sapped your physical energy, interfered with mental focus, or even threw you out of alignment with your highest purpose. If the challenges went on long enough, maybe you even experienced negative changes to your physical health.

While it's each person's responsibility to manage their own personal energy to best navigate difficult dynamics (our Energy Me Work), energy is a two-way street. Yes, the personal energy we bring to work affects the culture—but it's just as true that the culture deeply influences our personal energy, for better or worse depending on where culture falls on the accidental to intentional culture continuum (see Figure 4.1).

When we do our We Work, these negative impacts on energy and well-being are reduced or disappear. We can mentally focus on what's most important instead of the unresolved drama; we feel more emotionally resilient; and we can attend to our own needs consistently, so we maintain strong physical health and alignment with purpose.

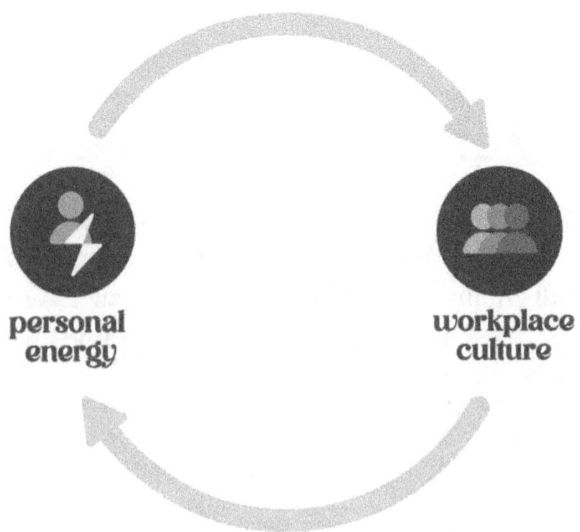

FIGURE 4.1 Personal energy and workplace culture.

When done well, We Work shifts the collective energy of the group in a way that allows us to fulfill our team's potential. We move:

From	**To**
Withdrawn or checked out	Engaged and willing
Withholding	Revealing
Frustrated or angry	Relieved and satisfied
Cynical	Hopeful and optimistic
No humor or biting sarcasm	Good-spirited humor
Armored and self-protecting	Open and vulnerable
Emotionally reactive	Emotionally responsive

Think about the difference in these emotional states. Can you imagine how a team stuck in the left column will have trouble collaborating, innovating, learning, and problem-solving together? And how much productivity, performance, and results would improve if the team shifts to more right column energetic states? This is the impact of collective energy on both culture and organizational performance.

Connection

When the collective energy of a team shifts in a positive direction, it naturally paves the way for deeper human connection—the kind that can only grow when trust and openness replace tension and guardedness.

When we do our We Work well, we ultimately build trust through shared vulnerability, deepened mutual understanding, and a strengthened sense of belonging that keeps people invested in each other's success. Over time, these strengthened relationships become part of our team's cultural fabric, shaping how we communicate, collaborate, and show up for one another. When we are rooted in connection, we are more resilient in the face of challenges, generous in our assumptions about others, and more creative in problem-solving—because we know we are working *with* each other, not just alongside each other.

While designing workplaces that *feel better* is an important outcome in itself, this isn't just about feelings. There's an important link to organizational performance that can't be overstated. Teams who attend to their collective energy and nurture connection with each other *perform better together*, too.[1] In Chapter 7, we'll dig more deeply into this idea.

Courage

The combination of elevated collective energy and prioritizing strong connection with each other results in perhaps the most important factor in a team's ability to design, redesign, and maintain an intentional culture: courage.

When we know we are seen, valued, and supported, we are more willing to speak up, share a bold idea, admit a mistake, or challenge an assumption. These actions often require courage because they usually carry a risk: the risk of being misunderstood, creating conflict, standing out, being perceived as difficult or less valuable, being overlooked for promotion, or even being fired. But in a team that has invested in We Work, we are more likely to take these risks because we have greater confidence that our team members will support us if one of our fears does come true.

This isn't to say that choosing courage always goes the way we hope it will. There are times when making the courageous choice leaves us feeling vulnerable and unsupported. In those times, if we have done our Me Work, we are more able to maintain resilience and stick with courage because we are deeply connected to integrity and our personal values.

What Do You Do When Vulnerability Goes Wrong?

During the COVID-19 pandemic, I (Natalie) facilitated many trainings virtually. Some of our clients really leaned in, investing in their leaders to better equip them for the tough and disconnected times we were living in. I was working with a large federal government client. They prioritized a focus on courage, and I had the privilege of guiding more than 15 cohorts of their leaders through a multi-class experience on courageous leadership.

In one of those cohorts, all but one of the participants were men. As we explored the connection between courage and vulnerability, I noticed the only woman in my group start to raise her hand, then quickly pull it back down. Her hesitation caught me. I gently asked if she'd like to share. She paused, then spoke with a quiet steadiness: "I believe in courage and vulnerability. I try to practice it often, but it's really hard in my environment. What do you do when vulnerability goes wrong?"

I asked her to say more. She took a breath and continued, "Just like today, I'm often the only woman in the room. I want to share my thoughts and ideas, but I worry someone will laugh or use my words against me. Sometimes I speak up anyway and then it happens. Someone makes fun of me, or they use what I say against me. What do you do when your vulnerability goes wrong?" The virtual room went still. Her question landed heavily, pulling everyone into the reality of her experience.

It was a great question.

I told her, "Being brave doesn't mean it always goes well. Some of the most courageous people carry scars because they chose to be brave, knowing they couldn't control the outcome. Courage is about remembering why you did the difficult thing. You choose to be vulnerable and uncomfortable, because you are leaning into your values and your integrity. Although vulnerability feels like fear to you, it looks like courage to others. It's also really important to notice who is choosing to be brave with you and who is not. The critics aren't the brave ones. Real change begins when we step into discomfort together. That's We Work."

Months later, I learned what had grown out of that moment. Her courage hadn't just changed her experience; it began to shift the group. When she spoke up, others did too. Over time, the team became more open, more willing to take risks, and more committed to creating space for every voice. Gradually, vulnerability was less perceived as weakness and more as a spark that made the work stronger. That's the heart of We Work: when courage moves from being an individual practice to a collective one. This woman's brave comment was the catalyst for this team discovering a different kind of culture, where courage wasn't rare but frequent and shared.

Just like with energy and connection, courage has a compounding effect. One person or one team's brave act in the face of vulnerability can influence cultural norms more broadly. Over time, the group becomes more comfortable facing the uncomfortable—naming problems, addressing tensions, and making changes that matter.

What Is Your Team's We Work?

First, let's clarify how to think about the word "team."

As you complete this assessment, it will be important to think about a specific group of people. You are welcome to complete the assessment multiple times with different groups of people in mind. For example, if you are an executive leader of an organization with different teams and many direct reports, you might choose to think about several different teams, one at a time:

- The executive leadership team you are a member of
- You and the top-level leaders who report directly to you
- Your entire department or unit

If you are an individual contributor in your organization, you might think about either:

- All the colleagues in your department or unit, or
- The smaller group of people you work most closely with

No matter where you sit in your organization, if you are part of a nuclear family with any drama or dysfunction, you might find it interesting to take this assessment thinking about your family unit as well. (Is there a family in existence that does *not* have drama or dysfunction?)

No matter what you identify, this assessment is not an indictment of your team's dysfunction or cultural norms and there is no need to get stuck in shame or judgment. All teams need We Work to fulfill their potential. This assessment is simply information—a way to laser in your thinking on where your team needs We Work so you can be a catalyst for that work or at least helpfully support it.

Identify Your Team's We Work

The following are examples of We Work your team might take on together—not as one-time fixes, but as intentional practices that strengthen relationships, improve group functioning, and steadily shape a healthier workplace culture. Check the box beside any idea that would be helpful for you to do with one other person, or a few, or with your entire team.

- ☐ **Improve communication**
  - ☐ Meet to develop shared agreement on desired communication norms. Together, answer questions such as: *What communication norms exist on our team that are healthy and should be nurtured and rewarded? What norms do we want to change?*
  - ☐ From this discussion, establish or recommit to communication guidelines. Make sure these guidelines are reinforced visually in places people will see them (i.e., wall posters, table tents, etc.).
  - ☐ Learn together about important communication fundamentals such as compassionate candor, listening with intention, asking powerful questions, tone and body language, etc.
  - ☐ Commit to and practice generating empathy for each other more often.
  - ☐ Commit to and practice listening with helpful intentions instead of the intention to reply.
  - ☐ Commit to and practice compassionate candor.
  - ☐ Commit to and practice sharing feedback directly and with care.
  - ☐ Commit to and practice reducing defensiveness.
  - ☐ Other: ______________________________.
- ☐ **Clarify expectations or guidelines to reduce confusion, uncertainty, or friction** (If you check this one, write here what specifically needs clarity and shared agreement, then review the rest of the bullets in this section with that in mind):

  ____

  - ☐ If necessary, gather feedback from the team about their confusion, uncertainty, or friction with a survey or in one-to-one or small group conversations to ensure the group's needs are addressed.

- ☐ Meet with the purpose of clarifying expectations or guidelines as a starting point for shared agreement; be sure the purpose of the meeting is clearly communicated to team members, there is an established agenda shared with everyone, and the meeting is facilitated by someone who has the skill and confidence to lead the conversation well.
- ☐ After verbal clarity and shared agreement has been established, discuss what systems or accountability mechanisms may need to be established or recommitted to that will keep people acting in accordance with the expectations or guidelines (for example, a recurring meeting agenda item for regular check-ins, communication with other teams, boundaries with technology, etc.).
- ☐ After verbal clarity and shared agreement has been established, create written or visual reinforcement such as a follow-up email, a new or refined process document shared with the team, printed expectations for a breakroom wall, etc.
- ☐ Other: ______________________________

☐ **Increase inclusion and belonging**[2]

- ☐ Commit to learning together about these concepts: what they mean, how they influence culture and performance, and how each person can help.
- ☐ Start meetings with structured or unstructured personal connection so that team members stay in touch with each other as people, not just colleagues.
- ☐ Ensure that new members of the team are given opportunities to get to know each other through introductions, time spent together, etc.
- ☐ Rotate meeting facilitation so more voices are in visible leadership roles.
- ☐ Audit team events (i.e., meetings, celebrations, social gatherings) to ensure they reflect the diversity of the group's interests and needs and that they are organized around inclusive practices.

- ☐ Make space in meetings for everyone to contribute—for example, use a "round robin" check-in or written input method.
- ☐ Other: ______________________________

☐ **Increase candor and direct conversation**

- ☐ Learn together about the concept of candor: why it's important, why it's hard, and how to increase candor among members of your team. (We'll dig deeply into the topic of candor in Chapter 8.)
- ☐ Develop shared language to help people speak more directly to each other and commit to using this language with each other.[3]
- ☐ Commit to and practice "truth with kindness" by giving constructive feedback in the moment rather than letting issues simmer.
- ☐ Commit to and practice using shared discussion tools, like "I notice/I wonder," to bring up observations without assigning blame.
- ☐ Other: ______________________________

☐ **Improve the team's ability to learn efficiently**

- ☐ Discuss together the current norms, system issues, and other obstacles that make it difficult for members of the team to learn at or faster than the pace of change. Decide as a group how you'll address the obstacles that the team has control over.
- ☐ After completing a project, hold a short "what we learned" debrief before moving on.
- ☐ Purposefully allocate time to talk about mistakes through the lens of learning and growth.
- ☐ Practice admitting when we don't know or need help so that others can support us.
- ☐ Identify and eliminate obstacles that prevent knowledge from effectively being shared across the team.
- ☐ Other: ______________________________

- ☐ **Empower full contribution**
  - ☐ Discuss together the current norms, system issues, and other obstacles that make it difficult for members of the team to contribute as fully as they can. Decide as a group how you'll address the obstacles that the team has control over.
  - ☐ Engage in a facilitated session designed to identify and leverage team members' personalities, strengths, and preferred working styles. Follow this session with mechanisms for ensuring this has lasting impact such as easily accessible reminders of each person's strengths, styles, and personalities.
  - ☐ Enact processes in meetings that invite quieter people to share their ideas.
  - ☐ Use brainstorming techniques that allow for both spoken and written contributions.
  - ☐ Pair team members with complementary strengths on projects to unlock untapped skills.
  - ☐ Invite team members to share one "stop, start, continue" idea in regular reflection sessions.
  - ☐ Other: ______________________________
- ☐ **Encourage challenging the status quo**
  - ☐ Learn together about the different types of conflict and how best to navigate conflict together.
  - ☐ Discuss our learning with each other and develop common language to help us challenge the status quo and commit to using this language with each other.
  - ☐ Schedule a quarterly "fresh eyes" review of processes, asking, "If we were starting from scratch, how would we do this?" or "What's another way to think about X?"
  - ☐ Other: ______________________________
- ☐ **Build or rebuild trust**
  - ☐ Together, learn a model for discussing trust that makes the concept less threatening.

- ☐ Create and post easily accessible visuals that remind team members about this model[4] and encourage them to talk about it in these less threatening terms.
- ☐ Together, define what vulnerability might look like for our team, with specific examples. Practice vulnerability with each other and reflect on lessons.
- ☐ Engage in an interactive facilitated discussion together designed to encourage each team member to reflect on how they may be undermining trust with one or more people in the group and to learn strategies for building and repairing trust.
- ☐ Build opportunities for people to address trust issues with each other in 1:1 meetings.
- ☐ Create opportunities for informal connection to humanize relationships outside of work such as social events, having lunch together regularly, etc.
- ☐ Other: ________________________________

☐ **Make meetings more effective**

- ☐ Discuss together what's working well with meetings and what needs to be improved. Cultivate a list of improvement needs for meetings, get to alignment on priority changes, and assign responsibility for making these improvements.
- ☐ Identify an established and proven model for effective meetings the team can follow and commit to using this structure; assign responsibilities for implementing this structure over time.[5]
- ☐ Begin with a clear purpose and desired outcome for every meeting.
- ☐ Use agendas that include time limits and ownership for each item; ensure there is an easy way for team members to add items to the agenda.
- ☐ Ensure team meetings have an identified facilitator with the skills and confidence to keep the meeting on track and in alignment with agreed-upon structure. If no one on the

team feels they can do this well, invest in training and development for at least one person to fill this facilitator role.

- ☐ Ensure meetings include a section at the end where clarity is established on decisions, ownership, timelines, and cascading messages.
- ☐ End each meeting with a meeting rating effectiveness tool like a simple 1–10 scale.
- ☐ Other: ____________________

☐ **Increase accountability**

- ☐ Discuss together where the team is doing a great job with accountability and where there are gaps. Cultivate a list of improvement needs and assign responsibility for addressing these needs.
- ☐ Together, learn a model for thinking about accountability that includes language the entire team can learn and use on a daily basis. (Chapter 10 is all about accountability.)
- ☐ Define clear ownership and expectations for each other so nothing "falls between the cracks."
- ☐ Practice speaking candidly to each other about accountability gaps and missed commitments using non-threatening language.
- ☐ Set regular check-in points for progress updates.
- ☐ Other: ____________________

☐ **Reduce technology overload or distraction/improve collective mental focus**

- ☐ Discuss together the current norms, system issues, and other obstacles that make it difficult for members of the team to stay focused and carve out time for uninterrupted work. Decide as a group how you'll address the obstacles that the team has control over.
- ☐ Agree on "quiet hours" or meeting-free blocks for deep work.
- ☐ Limit internal email or messaging outside agreed-upon hours.
- ☐ Consolidate communication channels to reduce the need to check multiple platforms.

- ☐ Periodically schedule a team check-in on this issue and make refinements based on feedback.
- ☐ Other: ____________________________

☐ **Reduce gossip or back channeling**

- ☐ Invite people into conversation about the gossip or back channeling that exists with the aim to create shared agreement that feedback about someone should be brought directly to them (or their supervisor if appropriate) rather than discussed with others.
- ☐ In meetings, invite questions or concerns to be verbalized aloud—either in the meeting or with you individually afterward—to reduce the need for gossip or "the meeting after the meeting."
- ☐ Create clear, safe pathways for surfacing concerns so people feel less need to vent privately.
- ☐ Decide together how you agree to handle situations where one person experiences another person gossiping or sharing information that is not theirs to share. Explore the difficulties of doing so and normalize the challenge associated with this. Establish language to make this easier to do with each other.
- ☐ Other: ____________________________

Worth Repeating

Now that you've identified We Work that needs to be done, how are you feeling? Energized? Overwhelmed? Focused? Unsure where to start? Whatever you're feeling, it's normal.

At the same time, you'll be most effective at doing and supporting We Work if you keep a few ideas in mind to maintain perspective, clarity, and optimism. These ideas will sound familiar because you read a version of them in Chapter 3. But here they are again, nuanced for We Work:

1. **Adaptive versus technical:** As you are considering We Work and discussing it with people on your team, try to assess whether the work is an adaptive challenge or a technical one so that you are realistic

about what it will take and where "solutions" might come from. Most big changes will include both: elements that can be addressed with fairly simple technical fixes and other elements that will require a significant shift in individuals' beliefs, thinking patterns, emotional reactions, and decision-making models.

2. **Prioritize:** Look again at the We Work assessment. What stands out to you as either: a) low-hanging fruit ideas you could get quick traction with, and b) ideas that may be harder or more complex but that will be great ROI to your team culture? Choose one, two, or at most three items from your list and make those your starting point.
3. **Progress, not perfection:** Reminder: Perfection isn't necessary—or possible. Culture work simply asks us to do better for ourselves and each other *more of the time*. As you embark upon We Work with your team, pay attention to when there is even the tiniest bit of progress, acknowledge it out loud, and celebrate it. Our human brains tend to have unrealistic expectations and be overly focused on what's wrong versus what's right or going well. Notice if that happens to you and keep yourself focused on where this is progress, what's next, and what's within your sphere of control. Setbacks are a normal part of the process and to be expected. We Work is an ongoing evolution, not a one-and-done effort.
4. **Why this matters:** If you have the sense that this We Work is starting to sound like "group therapy" and wondering again . . . why does this matter? What does all this have to do with culture or organizational performance? No problem. Let's revisit the formula again, as often as we need to:

Workplace culture is the result of collective group norms. > Norms are the result of individual behaviors interacting with each other. > To change norms, we need:

- individuals to change their own behaviors, which requires Me Work, and we need
- individuals to change the way they *relate* with each other, which requires We Work.

5. **The bonus benefit:** Here's the good news again: All the learning, effort, and adaptation you put into We Work with your team is *directly transferrable* elsewhere; it's never a waste of time. Even if you find another job, you get to bring the personal benefits of We Work with you—to the next job and to your personal relationships.

You—Yes YOU!

If you're a formal leader with direct reports, you may now easily see many opportunities for yourself to be a catalyst for or even actively lead We Work on your team. As we'll talk about in Chapter 6, you are the cultural architect on your team. You not only have the option and privilege of heavily influencing cultural norms by doing your own Me Work and leading We Work, *it is your responsibility to do so*. If you want to be a great leader, you must take this responsibility to heart and act on it. If you don't want this responsibility as part of your daily work life, then you may want to reconsider your role.

But what if you're not a formal leader and you don't have any direct reports?

Pay attention—this matters!

As we said in Chapter 3 . . . you have agency. Despite the fact that formal leaders can have the *most* influence on cultural norms because of their positional power, every one of us influences culture every single day by how we show up and relate with each other. It does not matter what you do in your organization. If you interact with anyone for even the smallest amount of time, you influence culture.

So how do you take that truth—that you influence culture every day—and turn it into action? You don't need a title or a budget to spark We Work. You just need the courage to notice what would help your team thrive and the willingness to take small, intentional steps. Here are a few practical ways to exercise your personal agency and become a catalyst for improving culture norms on your team through We Work.

1. **Demonstrate the behaviors you want to see.**
   If you want more openness, be the first to share ideas or admit mistakes. If you want more appreciation, express gratitude often. People notice patterns, and behaviors tend to ripple outward.
2. **Start with small, human moments.**
   Invite a teammate to lunch, initiate a quick "good news" round in a meeting, or greet people by name when you pass them. While people often think of "culture change" as a grand, sweeping organizational initiative, cultures change by small shifts in everyday actions.
3. **Ask powerful, team-oriented questions.**
   Look for opportunities in meetings, small group conversations, or 1:1 interactions where you might ask questions that spark curiosity, willingness, or motivation. Using inquiry more than telling is a great behavior to model and often leads to deeper connection, greater understanding,

and better solutions. You might ask "What's at the heart of this challenge we are having?" or "How can I be helpful here?" Check out our list of Powerful Questions on our website for examples you might use.

4. **Be a connector.**
   If you see gaps between groups or roles, introduce people to each other, share helpful information, and connect dots others might not see. Take initiative for connecting people to people, ideas to ideas, and people to ideas.
5. **Offer to facilitate, not dominate.**
   When you spot an area where We Work could help, say: "Would it be helpful if I set up a quick brainstorm so we can align?" This keeps the focus on the team's needs, not just your own.
6. **Celebrate progress out loud.**
   When your team makes even small steps toward better collaboration, acknowledge it. Recognition reinforces the behavior you want to see. If someone admits a mistake in a meeting and you know that was a vulnerable act for them, you can quietly but powerfully reward that behavior by saying something like "Thanks for sharing that mistake, Rich. That was helpful for me because I now understand something I didn't before."
7. **Be a safe harbor.**
   Create one-on-one moments where people feel they can share concerns or ideas without fear of judgment. Often, trust between individuals is the seed for broader We Work.
8. **Share credit generously.**
   Frequently acknowledge others' contributions out loud in group settings. This not only strengthens relationships but encourages a culture of mutual respect.

Free resources available at www.vidlwork.com/culturejourneybook

- List of Powerful Questions to support We Work
- "Rumble Language" from Brene Brown
- List of our favorite books, many of which support We Work, including all the books referenced in the endnotes
- List of our favorite podcasts, many of which support We Work
- Link to the Level 10 Meeting Agenda from EOS

5 System Issues

"More Stress Management?"

I (Natalie) am in conversation with Holly, a leader with one of our large government clients. We're discussing training we might offer their people leaders this year. Holly says, "I know I sound like a broken record, but I think we need more training on stress management. Our climate survey results are in and—no surprise—people are reporting feeling higher levels of stress than ever. What do you have on stress management?"

Holly shared the results of the climate survey with me prior to this conversation so I'm prepared for this. I know the data highlights several issues that are creating stress for employees. Comments from the survey include "too much bureaucracy," "excessive red tape," and "hiring takes forever." Common sentiments in the survey include "I'm at the mercy of people at the top of the hierarchy" and "I feel like I have no control."

I decide to take the conversation in a different direction than Holly might be expecting:

"We can absolutely offer another round of training on stress reduction. But I think we should dig a little deeper and talk about what's at the heart of the high stress levels. Think about you and your own team for a minute. The red tape, excessive paperwork, decisions and hiring taking forever . . . you're experiencing these same issues, right? And how do they leave you feeling?"

Holly nods her head yes and says without missing a beat: "Desperate! Frustrated. And like I just want to give up."

I ask her: "Would a stress management training be helpful to you right now?"

Holly replies, "The stress management training we did two years ago was valuable because it reminded me to focus on what I have control over and to reframe stressors. I continue to work on that. But there's only so much I can do when I feel like I'm drowning in big issues that we can't seem to resolve. What I really need is to feel like someone *understands* how difficult these circumstances are. And I feel like we need to be able to talk more openly and learn to respond differently. Right now, we're all just complaining to each other—but no one's really trying to communicate the need for change or influence the problems for the better."

Now Holly and I are having the conversation we need to have.

We've just made an important shift so that we're no longer talking only about Me Work; we're finally talking about structural problems and the We Work necessary to best respond to them. This is good because I know that this organization's leaders need more significant support than another training on stress management. What they need is for the agency to attend to the big organizational systems and structures that are undermining culture and performance—and to help teams change the way they respond to the ones that can't be fully resolved. In essence, they need help with their system issues.

What Are System Issues?

System issues are the challenges or circumstances that exist within or outside of the team or organization that contribute to friction, confusion, or toxicity. System issues typically fall into one of three categories:

1. Out of our control, unresolvable, and without a clear end in sight; for example:
   - regulatory changes
   - rapid industry change
   - global climate change

2. Temporary and, while not immediately resolvable, at least partially within the organization's control; for example:
   - a company merger or acquisition
   - implementation of new IT systems
   - significant employee shortages due to turnover or unfilled positions
3. Resolvable, but requiring significant decisions and effort by more than one person; for example:
   - outdated company policies
   - ineffective leadership structures that could be adjusted
   - too many communication channels without adequate guidelines for use
   - outdated, ineffective, or nonexistent accountability processes

You might notice in the first category, all the examples end with the word "change." The exponential rate of change in our world today is itself an unresolvable system issue. And it brings with it other system issues, such as steep technology learning curves, frequent market disruptions, and overwhelmed and under-skilled leaders struggling to lead their teams effectively.

System issues are normal and to be expected. No team or organization exists without them. But, when not properly addressed, they can undermine culture and an organization's ability to retain its top talent and fulfill its potential. They do this by draining energy from people, distracting them from shared goals, making daily work harder, and creating an environment where frustration and mistrust grow. Over time, unresolved system issues normalize dysfunction, making it harder for even the most well-intentioned people to sustain a healthy, intentional culture.

The good news is that, while no team can eliminate system issues entirely, they can learn to face them openly, respond with creativity, and build resilience together. This starts by acknowledging system issues as shared challenges to be faced together rather than as immovable obstacles or failures to be blamed on someone.

Norms Versus System Issues

It's important to know the difference between system issues and group norms. While both system issues and unhelpful group norms can create friction, confusion, and underperformance, they are not the same thing and require a slightly different type of attention.

System issues exist independently of group norms and often have to do with circumstances outside of any one person or team's control. You might think of system issues as stormy weather hanging over the team or organization.

Let's think about this through the lens of the client we just described:

One of the *giant* system issues that exists is the size and structure of the organization itself: tens of thousands of employees in a large, siloed hierarchy with a history of command-and-control style leadership. This giant system issue creates other system issues like excessive "red tape" and long wait times to get basic decisions made. When these system issues and their effects are not proactively attended to, they begin to erode culture.

In the case of this client (and many others we've worked with), these system issues were *worsened* by ineffective group norms surrounding the system issues. For example, the general tendency for employees in this agency in response to these system issues was to:

- assume the worst
- not push for clarity when they needed it
- complain about it to other people
- disengage from work because of it
- allow themselves to exist in chronically high levels of personal stress

Of course, not every single employee was doing all of the above things. But that was the *pattern* we learned about, *especially on the teams where the formal leader was not fully embracing their role as cultural architect.*

While the system issues in this organization were deep and may not change quickly (or ever), these unhelpful group norms *are not the only response option—and ultimately make the system issues worse.* What if, instead, people on certain teams collectively committed to:

- assume positive intent
- ask for clarity when they need it
- talk directly to people instead of about them
- take 100% responsibility for whatever they have control over
- practice strategies that allowed them to periodically complete the stress response and emotionally reset

You can imagine how the environment on that team would be more enjoyable to work in despite the frustrating system issues—and how that team would have the best chance of influencing change over time.

What's key to remember here is this:

Evolving group norms are always something a group can do *if* they collectively choose to change them by intentionally doing their Me Work and We Work. While the existence of system issues may be outside the group's sphere of control, how they agree to behave in response to system issues makes all the difference.

How Do We Respond to System Issues?

This is a good time to think about an important concept called "the sphere of control."

At any given moment in the midst of any circumstance, each one of us is focusing and expending our physical, mental, emotional, and even spiritual energy in one direction or another. Where we direct our energy can be generally categorized in three ways: things we *cannot* control, things we *might* be able to influence, and things we *can* control (see Figure 5.1).

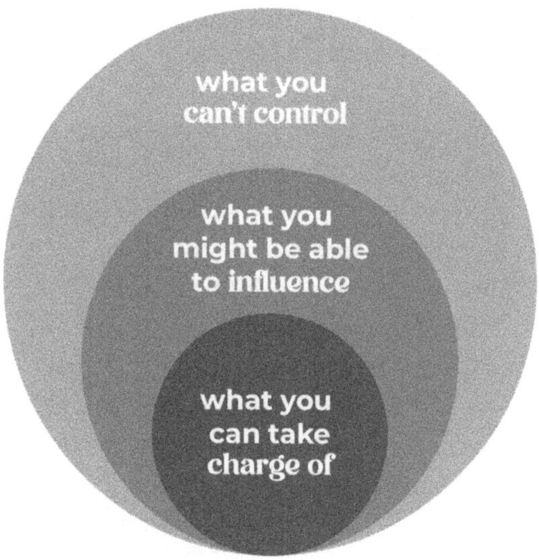

FIGURE 5.1 Sphere of control.

When we direct our energy toward things that are out of our control, we not only voluntarily increase our own stress response, but we also undermine our own power and potential for influence. Energy focused on things we cannot control is wasted time and energy.

What is in the realm of things we cannot control?

A lot.

As much as we might like to, we cannot control our colleagues or our boss or the people we serve. We cannot control our partners, our parents, our children, our siblings, our friends, our neighbors, or strangers. We cannot control the weather or the federal interest rate or our organization's hierarchy or anything that has already occurred in the past.

To be most effective and connected in life—and, thus, in the workplace—it's our responsibility to pay attention to where we are directing our energy. When we notice we are focused on, ruminating about, or complaining about things we cannot control, we can *decide* to recapture that precious energy and direct it toward the things we can control.

What is 100% within our control?

You guessed it. For each of us, the answer to this question is the same.

Only me.

I am in control of me—my thoughts, emotional responses, decisions, actions, and reactions. You are in control of you—your thoughts, emotional responses, decisions, actions, and reactions.

The good news about this situation is this:

When we become more skilled and practiced at taking charge of our inner operating system and our behaviors, several things happen. First, we notice we feel less stressed and our quality of life increases. Second, our relationships improve because we stop inadvertently disconnecting ourselves from others by micro-managing to control, or reacting defensively in response to feeling out of control. Third, we actually *become* a person of greater influence. When we take charge of ourselves well, we become a person who others want to listen to, be influenced by, have confidence in, and support. We become a stronger change maker not by focusing energy on the things we cannot control—but by consistently directing our energy toward what we can control, which is always and only us. Let's look at the sphere of control again with some added context (see Figure 5.2).

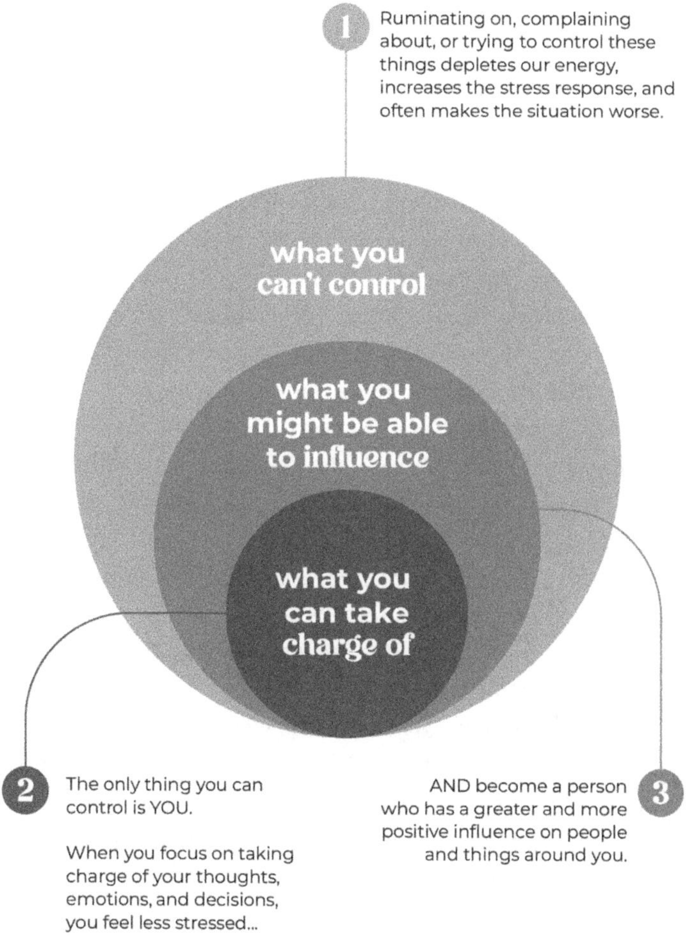

FIGURE 5.2 Explaining the sphere of control.

Issues that are out of our control and unresolvable

With system issues that are completely out of our control and unresolvable, our priority is to adapt as well as possible. If we cannot make a challenge go away, our next best option is to thoughtfully and proactively decide how we're going to respond—and then act in accordance with those decisions. This starts by identifying what we have control over.

For example, if your team is imminently at risk of a funding cut that no one in the organization can prevent or change, your team likely cannot control if the funding cut happens and you likely cannot control if your job or projects will be affected.

Personally, you can control:

- *How you think about the situation:* Do you allow yourself to ruminate on worst-case scenarios and catastrophize or do you decide to pay extra attention to your own narratives and assumptions to make sure they are based in fact and solutions?
- *What you do with your emotions:* It's natural to feel uncomfortable emotions like worry, frustration, and anger when we're being negatively affected by circumstances out of our control. But what we decide to do when these emotions arise is within our control. Do you react unproductively or repress the emotions with unhealthy coping mechanisms—or do you process the emotions and practice strategies to reset?
- *How you talk with others about the situation:* Do you engage in drama promoting and gossip conversations that keep the team stuck in worry mode? Or do you become the catalyst for candid, solutions-focused conversations with team members to adapt quickly and figure out how you'll collectively navigate the new budget?
- *What you do:* Do you wait for other people to take charge of the situation or figure things out? Or do you research how other organizations have handled similar situations, connect with colleagues who might be able to help, and bring ideas up for consideration to the team?

By taking charge of YOU, you might be able to **influence** important variables and outcomes like:

- Other team members' attitude and energy—because energy is contagious
- The collective decisions that are eventually made
- Which projects get prioritized
- How quickly your team successfully adapts

Issues that are temporary and partially within our control

With the second type of system issues—those are temporary and partially within our control—our priority is to influence or change what we can and then adapt to the rest as well as possible. These system issues also invite us to ask individually and collectively: *What is within our control right now? Where do we have influence? What can we change? How do we need to adapt?*

For example, let's say your organization is in the midst of a significant IT upgrade. You are the leader of a department, and your team members are reporting frustration over slower systems and frequent glitches. Instead of letting frustration dominate and excessive complaining undermine morale, you'll need to take charge of whatever you can control. For example, you could:

- Meet with the IT leader to ensure she has received feedback from your team and is aware of the problems
- With your team, commit to a short, daily "pulse check" to share concerns and updates
- Adjust work plans, goals, and expectations as necessary
- Encourage humor to lighten the mood
- Keep this situation in perspective and stay out of victim thinking
- Help your team members do the same

While these things don't make the system issue vanish, they do help the team preserve morale and stay in collaboration with each other.

Issues that are resolvable but require significant action by people in formal leadership roles

Some system issues require more than adaptation and focus on our sphere of control; they need decisions and actions from leaders who have influence over policies, structures, or resources. If you are a formal leader with the ability to partially or completely resolve a system issue, you *must* own this responsibility and do whatever is within reason to do. Otherwise, you are abdicating responsibility. If left unchecked, resolvable system issues unnecessarily erode morale and undermine culture quickly. If you're serious about culture change, you must get serious about resolving system issues.

Let's say you are part of an executive leadership team, and you are aware that employees in your organization are frustrated by a sense of inequity around how remote work policies are enforced. In some regions and under some leaders, no one is allowed to work from home except in emergency circumstances. In other places, employees work from home more than they come into the office. And in other regions it's somewhere in between, with no apparent consistency across the board. This is creating friction among employees.

If remote work policy falls under your jurisdiction, you must be the catalyst for resolving this issue sooner rather than later. It is your responsibility to address the issue with your colleagues, gather input if you need to, ensure thoughtful decisions are made, communicate these decisions to the organization, and implement mechanisms for ensuring consistent application across regions. Of course, you wouldn't make all this happen by yourself; resolving this system issue will require collaboration across departments. But if you are leading the team where accountability for this issue resides, it is your responsibility to lead others to get to resolution. If you are *not* the leader who is accountable for this issue but you are aware this issue needs attention, you are called to action: speak candidly about it and be the catalyst for momentum.

If you are not a leader who has enough influence to be the catalyst for resolving this issue, your job is to revert to focusing on what you *do* have control over and helping your team members do the same.

What System Issues Are Impacting Your Team?

Now is an opportunity to identify the system issues that are impacting you and your work team. This will require some written reflection.

Don't skip this part! If you're like most people who do this activity, you'll find it illuminating and hopeful.

Step 1: Identify system issues.

In the blank space below, make a list of the system issues that are negatively impacting you or your team. Think about circumstances larger than your team that are undermining culture or otherwise causing friction, confusion, or underperformance.

Step 2: Place the variables. Choose ONE from the list. Think about as many of the variables of this system issue as you can. Think about you, the other people involved, past events, future possibilities, outcomes, processes, etc. Place each variable in the column it belongs in. Is it 100% within your control? Write it in the left column. Is it totally out of your control? Write it in the right column. If it's something you *might* be able to influence, write it in the center.

Can Control	Might Influence	Cannot Control

Step 3: Make your commitment.
As you consider what you just wrote, reflect on these questions in writing.

In what ways am I wasting energy on things I cannot control?

If I was to redirect that energy toward things I CAN control, what would I do?

How can I influence change with this system issue, even if only in the smallest of ways?

To help resolve this system issue or support our team in better adapting to it, I commit to . . .

Me-We-Systems

We know now that system issues are best resolved or adapted to when we each take 100% responsibility for what is within our control and stop wasting energy on things we cannot. But there is one more crucial connection to make here:

> **Systems issues are also best resolved or adapted to by people who are doing their Me Work and We Work.**

If you are still challenged by the idea of deeply investing in self-development or relationship building on your team because it seems soft or "woo-woo," perhaps this idea makes it more concrete or digestible for you. Yes, Me Work and We Work make the workplace *feel better* and that is important because people *work better* when they feel better about themselves and each other. But another bottom line result of Me Work and We Work is that it helps us identify, address, and move through the inevitable challenges our teams and organizations will face. System issues will continue to arise as long as work exists. There is no end to them. If the race is to get and remain highly effective even as we face issue after issue, the fuel to get us there is Me Work and We Work (see Figure 5.3).

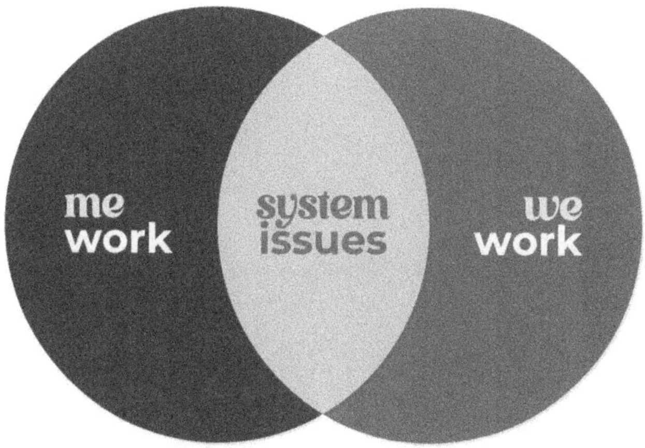

FIGURE 5.3 Me-We-Systems.

In Summary

Culture improves when we stop wasting energy on what we can't control and invest energy where it matters most. System issues will always exist, but how we respond to them individually (Me Work) and collectively (We Work) determines whether they erode culture or strengthen it. It's crucial to identify the system issues your team is facing. Name them specifically as the first step in resolving them or adapting to them as well as possible.

Then, we must decide where we have influence and move in that direction. In Chapter 6, we invite leaders to step fully into something they always have control over—the degree to which they take responsibility for their role as cultural architects, designing the structures, practices, and norms that allow people to thrive.

Are you ready to design the blueprints? Turn the page.

6 Leaders Are Cultural Architects

"Here We Go Again"

The room is quiet. I (Rebecca) can feel the hesitation hanging in the air. A dozen leaders shift in their seats, eyes down, avoiding mine. I have asked for someone to reflect on the conversations they were just having in their small groups. No one wants to speak first—not in front of the CEO. We're here to discuss one of the group's biggest system issues: competing goals. Every year, the Board sets its own priorities on top of the leadership team's goals, leaving them caught between two sets of expectations and an impossible workload.

Finally, Marla raises her hand and says softly, "This has been a problem for as long as I've been here. We're exhausted from trying to meet two sets of goals. Sometimes the Board's priorities pull us away from the real work we need to do. Our table was discussing whether there is a way to change the Board's process so it's not so hard on all of us."

Because of my previous experience with the team, I am aware that Marla's courage to say this out loud is monumental.

Heads nod and it's quiet again. Marty, the CEO, leans back in his chair and exhales. "I know I'm supposed to be working on being more open to ideas," he says, "but honestly? That's never going to happen. I don't see the Board changing."

I can feel the room deflate.

After a long pause, another leader, Joanne, nervously speaks up, her voice shaking. "Do you see it, Rebecca? This is what always happens. Someone finally speaks up, and they get shut down. Because of the work we've been doing with you, I've been hopeful this would change. But after hearing that, I just think . . . here we go again."

I turn to the CEO. "Marty, this is a moment that matters. Your team is giving you valuable feedback and they need you to listen. Can you try again?"

Marty pauses for a beat, sighs deeply, and finally says, "Okay. I understand this has been difficult, but I don't know how to fix this. The Board is very attached to providing input. But I hear you. I think we've all had a long day so let's put this at the top of the list for our next meeting. Send me your ideas on how we might solve this. I'll commit to reading them and considering our options."

Marty pauses and, just as I'm about to move the conversation along, he says one more small but important sentence: "Marla and Joanne, thank you for pushing on this."

The Power of Architects

Just as an architect's blueprints determine how a building is constructed, leaders' actions design and reinforce foundational elements in their team's culture. That's why we refer to formal leaders as "cultural architects." Because of their positional power—the power that comes from their title and role—formal leaders have an outsized influence on the daily experience of the people on their team, whether they intend to or not. The words they say, the tone they use, their body language, their actions and reactions, the policies they set . . . every behavior they demonstrate, reward, or discourage . . . it all becomes part of the "blueprint" that others use to understand what is valued, accepted, or at least tolerated.

In Marty's case, his influence on the culture of his leadership team was even greater than the typical company leader. He had led this organization for decades with a command-and-control leadership style that generated fear, rewarded overwork, and squelched candor and open discussion. Marty's perspective was that "you work as long as it takes to get the job done." He chronically worked long hours himself, without complaint, and expected nothing less from his direct reports.

Marty was also incredibly dedicated to the organization, his community, and his family. At heart, he was a kind person who was simply operating with outdated ideas about how best to lead. Importantly, he was also aware that the culture in his organization was mediocre and even toxic in some pockets. He was the impetus for the organization's decision to invest in culture transformation work.

At the start of our work, Marty was unaware how much culture transformation work would require from him personally. Like many leaders at his level, he didn't realize he was the most powerful cultural architect in the organization. He didn't understand how much influence his mindset and actions had on the daily lives and working experience of his team and how that trickled down through the rest of the organization. To his credit, he accepted the challenge with more grace and humility than most CEOs we've worked with: he was honest about his Me Work, engaged fully in professional coaching sessions, practiced new ways of relating with others in group sessions, and learned to receive feedback with a greater degree of openness.

While Marty happens to be a CEO, these truths apply to everyone in formal leadership. If you are a formal leader in your organization—meaning at least one person reports to you or considers you their "boss"—you are a cultural architect, *whether you want to be or not*. If you are not yet a formal leader but you aspire to be, this is important to know as you move into your first leadership role.

Like architecture, culture doesn't emerge by accident, it's built through countless small decisions and interactions that add up over time. Leaders who understand and are intentional about both the privileges and responsibilities of being a cultural architect influence culture positively through their everyday actions, big and small. Leaders who neglect this responsibility and either disengage or abuse their positional power are likely to find themselves leading dysfunctional teams with mediocre or toxic cultures.

Demonstrate, Reward, Discourage

As a cultural architect in your organization's CultureJourney, what are your tools?

When we work with leaders who are interested in or responsible for culture, we teach them that they have three primary tools for influencing culture. These tools come in the form of verbs: demonstrate, reward, and discourage.

Demonstrate

As a leader of a team, people are watching what you do. They are following your lead in determining what is rewarded, valued, accepted, or at least tolerated. Your actions are more important than your words; if there is incongruence between the two, people will pay attention to what you *do* more than what you *say*.

For example, if you want your team to ask better questions during meetings so learning, collaboration, and growth happens faster, what is the first thing you need to do? Ask more and better questions yourself. Demonstrate what curiosity looks like. Become a person who listens with helpful intentions.

If you want people to admit mistakes when they make them so that the team can learn collectively and reduce the likelihood of similar mistakes being made again, what is the most important thing you can do? Admit your mistakes publicly and engage in conversation with others about what you learned. Demonstrate what it looks like to handle mistakes with grace and use them as raw material for learning.

When it comes to culture, your first order of business as a leader is always to ensure you are modeling the characteristics, behaviors, and attitudes you want to cultivate on your team.

Reward

When we verbally or physically reward someone for their actions, it triggers neural pathways in their brain that connect the rewarded activity with a pleasant feeling. As humans, we do more of what we know will feel good and less of what we know will not. We are also always subconsciously looking for signs that we are accepted, approved, or that we belong—and rewarding someone signals acceptance, approval, and belonging.

For example:

Let's say there are two people on your team with a history of tension and unresolved conflicts. As a leader invested in improving workplace culture, what you *want* is for them be able to navigate their differences productively, in a way that prioritizes connection and courage over rightness, ego, or winning.

Perhaps you observe these two people in a meeting having a difficult conversation where they manage to successfully navigate their differences. They speak to each other directly, but with care, and reach a compromise that feels like a win-win for both. It is clear to you that these two people have done some important Me Work, and they are doing their We Work together in real time in this meeting.

This exchange should be acknowledged and rewarded, especially if it is a first for the two people.

Depending on the situation, you might choose to reward it publicly so that *other people* on the team also learn what is valued when it comes to differences and conflict. As the leader, you might say something during the meeting like:

> "Jamal and Paula, I know you both came to that conversation with different opinions and I appreciate how you navigated the tension in a way that led to the best resolution. Great work."

When it comes to culture, your second order of business as a leader is to be sure you are subtly, overtly, directly, and indirectly *rewarding* the attitudes, energy, thinking patterns, and choices that support the culture you are designing. Your priority is to acknowledge and reward Me Work, We Work, helpful behaviors, and productive resolution of system issues when you see them happening. Here are some other ways you might reward the behaviors, practices, and relational styles that support the desired culture:

- **Offer specific, private appreciation.** Take a moment to personally acknowledge what you saw or experienced, emphasizing the behaviors that mattered most.

- **Share the story with the larger team.** Retell the example (with permission) in a team meeting or written update as a way of reinforcing the behaviors and cultural norms you want to encourage.
- **Give visibility.** Highlight the person's contribution in front of senior leaders or other teams so their effort is recognized beyond the immediate group.
- **Encourage peer-to-peer recognition.** Invite other team members to share what they are noticing and appreciating, creating a ripple effect of acknowledgment.
- **Create growth opportunities.** Reward someone by asking them to lead a future project, facilitate a discussion, or mentor others, showing that their helpful behavior builds trust.
- **Celebrate informally.** Small gestures, like inviting them to share their perspective first in the next meeting or recognizing them in a lighthearted way (e.g., a team meeting shout-out), can go a long way.
- **Link behavior to values.** Point out how the action aligns with your team's stated values, helping people see the bigger cultural impact of what they did.
- **Offer symbolic tokens.** Use a rotating object (like a "team compass" or "culture coin") that is passed along when someone demonstrates behavior that elevates energy, prioritizes connection, or demonstrates courage.

Discourage

The third action leaders need to be thinking about as they are supporting other people in updating their iOS and relating with each other is *discourage*.

The hard truth is this: if there are attitudes and behaviors on your team that undermine the team's desired culture, those attitudes and behaviors *must be* respectfully but directly called out—and they must ultimately end. Full stop.

For example:

Let's say there is one member of your team who tends to gossip frequently and who shares information that is not theirs to share. You could choose to discourage this behavior in a number of ways:

- If you have not been explicitly clear with your entire team that gossiping is not accepted, you might bring this topic up in a team meeting and clearly set the expectation for everyone.
- You might meet with this one team member privately and say something like:

  "Jay, I want to discuss a behavior I've observed that I feel is unhelpful to our team. I often notice you talking with colleagues about other people's lives in a way that resembles gossip. On a couple of occasions, I've overheard you sharing information that is not yours to share. That concerns me because this behavior undermines trust on the team . . ."

  Continue the conversation from there, listening to Jay's perspective on this behavior, clarifying expectations, and challenging him to do better moving forward.

From our experience, most leaders find discouraging unwanted attitudes and behaviors to be the most challenging of the three actions. We often avoid proactively addressing unwanted behavior because:

- We don't like conflict, or anything that feels like conflict.
- We're worried about being perceived negatively or making other people uncomfortable.
- We're busy and think we don't have time or energy to dedicate to these types of conversations.

But, as Timothy Clark notes, "What you tolerate, you normalize."[1]

Tolerating unhelpful attitudes and behaviors undermines culture, decreases the morale and engagement of teams, and ultimately causes more frustration for the leader. If you don't spend a reasonable amount of time and energy discouraging incongruent behaviors as they arise, you will end up spending an unreasonable amount of time and energy stuck in the drama that ensues.

But What Will People Think?

When I (Natalie) think about how much influence a leader has on trust and the culture of an entire organization, I often think of one client, a government agency with a struggling culture. Many people dreaded coming to work, yet few ever left. The promise of pensions kept them tethered to jobs that drained them. Over time, the teams were filled with tension, reactivity, and burnout. It was a system stuck in survival mode.

I was brought in to coach their top leader, a smart, kind man who had spent his career serving others. He cared deeply about his people and his family, but he was running on empty. He wanted better health, more balance, and time for his wife, who was ill. We created small, realistic goals: breaks between meetings, regular exercise, more boundaries. But he rarely followed through. Every meeting was another conversation about how he didn't have time or the capacity to deliver on his personal health goals.

One day, I asked why he didn't use the state-of-the-art fitness center just a few floors below his office, the one he had personally approved. He looked horrified. "Could you imagine?" he said. "That fitness center has windows. If someone saw me exercising, I'd be on the front page of the newspaper tomorrow." He wasn't exaggerating. In that moment, I saw the deeper issue: in this man's mind, caring for himself at the "expense" of time away from work felt too risky. The culture equated exhaustion with dedication, and his fear was shaping everyone else's behavior. His silence was the signal to everyone else that self-care was not safe at work.

That realization changed our work. We started exploring the "what if." What if someone did see him? What if that moment became a message instead of a scandal? What if leadership meant showing that well-being wasn't weakness, but wisdom?

At first, he resisted. Then, slowly, he began to reframe what leadership could look like. He started occasionally scheduling walking meetings outside, declining a few back-to-back commitments, thanking the staff who ran the fitness center. He even shared his personal "why" with his executive team, how he wanted to be strong and supportive for his wife and the departments he oversaw. By the time I finished my work with this agency, the situation had shifted. He hadn't exactly become a poster child for the wellness program, but something real had changed. His team noticed. They began protecting their own energy, too. Some of them even used the fitness center more regularly. He had started modeling a different kind of strength, the kind that shows courage not through sacrifice, but through example. And that's how culture change begins, one brave action at a time. Every culture has its blueprint. Leaders draw and refine it, one choice at a time.

Demonstrate, Reward, Discourage: Self-Assessment

It's time to assess yourself. As always, the purpose of this assessment is *awareness, not judgment*. If you're honest with yourself, you'll likely find that you're already demonstrating, rewarding, and discouraging well in some areas with your team—and you'll see some opportunities for improvement.

Demonstrate	**Reward**	**Discourage**
What are you currently demonstrating that supports your desired team culture?	What are you currently rewarding to support your desired culture?	What are you currently discouraging to support your desired culture?

(Continued)

Demonstrate	Reward	Discourage
What do you *need to be* demonstrating better to support your desired culture?	What do you *need to be* rewarding more often to support your desired culture?	What do you *need to be* discouraging more often to support your desired culture?

Embracing Your Role

Being a cultural architect is both a privilege and a responsibility. Every interaction, every acknowledgment, and every boundary you set contributes to the story your team tells about what matters most. When leaders intentionally demonstrate and reward behaviors that are congruent with their desired culture—and discourage the opposite—they become a catalyst for turning the blueprint into the lived experience. But what exactly are you to be demonstrating, rewarding, and discouraging? We'll answer that question throughout the rest of this book.

7 Workplace Culture's Doppelganger

If someone tells you they've seen your doppelganger, it means they've seen a person who looks so much like you, they could be your twin, or at least your double on a movie set. Intentional workplace culture has a doppelganger—something that looks so similar, it's almost it's twin. That doppelganger is psychological safety. While they are not the same thing, they often look the same. If you are in a workplace where the culture feels healthy and intentional, it's very likely there is a high degree of psychological safety. And if you're in a culture that feels mediocre or toxic, it's likely there is much less of it.

The concept of psychological safety has become both more popular and more scrutinized in the last decade, with good reason. The research is clear that psychological safety is the *most essential ingredient* for effectively designing, building, maintaining, and repairing an intentional culture that supports people in fulfilling their potential and enables the organization to fulfill its mission.

We'll unpack the concept of psychological safety and make it highly actionable for you in this chapter. But first, a story.

"We've Been Through Hell"

We (the Vidl Work team) are working with a team of first responders from a fire department that has engaged us to assess their culture and make recommendations on how to improve it. We complete more than a dozen individual discovery conversations[1] with paramedics, firefighters, formal leaders, and administrators from the team. By the time we complete these sessions, we have heard several phrases over and over again, including: "Gotcha culture," "Command-and-control," "I have to protect myself," and "I don't trust [him, her, them]."

It makes sense that people are speaking in these terms because, over the last few years, they have been through what one first responder described simply as "hell." By many accounts, the department's previous Fire Chief was not fit for the level of power and responsibility of his role and behaved poorly in ways that negatively impacted others. Several employees were fired seemingly without adequate cause. Others were fast-tracked into assistant chief roles, perhaps prematurely or at least without having to progress through the traditional process. The sense among many on the team is that the previous Chief's personal preferences and loyalties determined who was hired, fired, promoted, or demoted. There have been multiple formal investigations, several of which have been public and embarrassing for the department.

In their discovery sessions, more employees than not described how this time has not only been bad for work, but it's also been extra hard on them personally because of how it has ruined relationships that used to exist outside of work. Prior to this intense drama and dysfunction, many first responders and their families were each other's primary social network. They hung out on their time off, their kids went to school together, and some even went to the same church. Over time, these tight social connections have been strained or have altogether dissolved into a disconnected, partisan, "us versus them" workplace where everyone feels they need to watch their back.

By the time we begin our work, the previous Chief has left and a new Fire Chief is leading the department. He is a very different type of leader—seemingly full of integrity, grit, and a genuine desire to return this fire department to its potential and willing to invest resources in outside support for help with culture. But he is new and the team is skeptical. Will he really be different? Only time will tell. Most people we talk with are barely at the level of cautious optimism; some are still understandably cynical.

As we look through the data from the discovery sessions, one thing becomes clear. This group of people is missing the most essential ingredient for achieving what the new Chief wants—and what, in reality, all of them want—a workplace that feels healthy and welcoming, the ability to trust each other again, and a fire department that can serve its community with excellence. That ingredient is psychological safety. On this team, there is none. Most people do not feel included except in their own small, protective cliques. Learning is nearly impossible. People are unable to contribute fully and there is no willingness to challenge the status quo for fear of repercussions. The current culture falls in the "toxic" range on the culture continuum.

Our experience has shown that first responders often work in environments where psychological safety is low, but this team is at rock bottom. Our work with them needs to start with the fundamentals: helping people feel safe enough to take the risks required to rebuild culture—and to ensure that courage and vulnerability can coexist.

A Brief Walk Down Memory Lane

While the phrase "psychological safety" feels new to many people, it is not at all a new concept. In fact, the language for this idea has been in existence for at least 70 years. Some sources suggest that the phrase "psychological safety" was first used by well-known therapist Carl Rogers in the 1950s. Whether he used that exact term or not, he did frequently use ideas that resemble it when writing about the conditions necessary for creativity and healing. In particular, Rogers described the need for environments where external evaluation is absent and where people feel empathetically understood.[2]

Around this same era, other scholars were exploring related ideas including Douglas McGregor in his work on the need for interpersonal trust.[3] In 1965, organizational development experts Edgar Schein and Warren Bennis discussed the concept in their writing as they described a climate "where one can take chances . . . without fear . . . thus a climate . . . that tolerates failure without retaliation . . ."[4]

Later, in 1990, William Kahn published a paper in which he explored how people need to feel psychologically safe to engage their full selves at work without fear of negative consequences to self-image, status, or career.[5]

In 1999, Amy Edmondson, then a student at Harvard Business School, published what has become known as a landmark paper titled *Psychological Safety and Learning Behavior in Work Teams*, which formally defines psychological safety as "a shared belief within a team that interpersonal risk is safe."[6] Edmondson's work on psychological safety since then is widely understood to have been the catalyst for moving the concept more fully into organizational research and practice. In 2012, Google embarked upon a four-year internal study to understand the difference between its higher and lower performing teams. This study, called *Project Aristotle*, moved the needle further as it placed psychological safety at the top of the list of most essential ingredients for high-performing teams.[7]

What Is Psychological Safety?

There are several accepted definitions of psychological safety, but we often start with the definition from Amy Edmondson's work, which defines the concept as:

> **A shared belief that the team environment is safe for taking interpersonal risks without fear of being punished, humiliated, or rejected.**

There is a lot to unpack in this definition. Here is a breakdown of a few key points worth underscoring:

- **Subjective:** Psychological safety is a *feeling* we get from other people about whether they are emotionally safe enough for us to take interpersonal risks. Each member of a team might have different internal evaluations and feelings about the degree of psychological safety based on their own internal narratives, their real-life experiences, and the nature of their relationships with others. People in a group with more social or professional privileges or power are more likely to assess an environment as psychologically safe than people with less. This means that each of us has the responsibility to do our best to *create* the conditions where others feel there is a high degree of psychological safety—but we cannot *make* another person believe the team is safe.

- **Interpersonal risks:** When we believe a high enough degree of psychological safety exists, it means we feel we can do things that we see as "interpersonally risky." Examples of interpersonal risks include admitting mistakes, asking for help, acknowledging that we don't know something, sharing a new idea, offering a dissenting opinion, or challenging the status quo. Depending on the people and circumstances, interpersonal risks might include even more basic behaviors such as making eye contact, greeting someone before they greet us, entering someone else's office, sharing something we found funny, or revealing a personal preference or value. The list of possible interpersonal risks is long because, ultimately, *most human interaction is vulnerable*—and risk is inherent in vulnerability.
- **Negative consequences:** What negative consequences are we afraid of that would prevent us from taking these risks if we determine the environment to be lacking in psychological safety? There are many. We might be afraid of subtle or overt changes in people's attitudes or evaluations about us—that people will judge in ways we don't want to be judged. For example, we might be concerned that others will think we are incompetent, unhelpful, annoying, "too much," a pain in the butt, not a team player, unrealistic, too rigid, too eager, overwhelmed, under-skilled . . . you name it. We might be concerned that these opinions of others will result in missing out on things we want, like a promotion, a raise, a new opportunity, people's respect and admiration, or feeling included in the group.

At the heart of it, the fears that prevent us from taking these interpersonal risks when psychological safety is low are all about *rejection*. Humans are biologically hard-wired to seek belonging in groups; it's an element of our evolutionary wiring that served us well eons ago when we might have literally died if we were rejected from our tribe. Most people in the workplace will only risk vulnerability when their internal assessment is that the chance of rejection is minimal—or when they have evolved their inner operating system enough to know they can emotionally handle the perceived or real rejection. The trouble is that the types of interpersonal risks we are describing here are *absolutely essential* for a high-performing team and thriving culture. When employees feel they need to be vigilantly protecting themselves instead of leaning into this type of human vulnerability, the team cannot be its best.

"It's Not My Job"

I (Rebecca) am facilitating a training with a group of leaders from a tech company. This group has been intentionally working on the culture within their own leadership group for several months. As with most of our clients, they learned about the concept of psychological safety early in our working relationship and we revisit the idea often.

In this conversation, we are talking about important diversity, equity, and inclusion work they are doing. One of the leaders suggests that perhaps there is not enough psychological safety on many teams so the tough conversations necessary for DEI work will be avoided or navigated with defensiveness—and thus the work will never fulfill its potential. I express my appreciation to this leader for recognizing the connection between psychological safety, tough conversations, and DEI work and expressing her opinion out loud.

Another leader, Derek, chimes in.

"I just can't get on board with this psychological safety thing. It's not my job to create safety for other people. I don't have time for that. I want to see *action* that makes this place feel better for people of color like me. We've been talking about equity for years—and yet nothing is different. How much longer are we going to have to wait?"

I feel relieved that Derek has finally said out loud what I suspected: he has not made the connection between psychological safety and the equity work that he is incredibly passionate about. This is a challenge because Derek is extremely influential, especially with other people of color in the organization. Without his recognition that psychological safety is necessary for this work, and his willingness to own his responsibilities in this area, he is inadvertently undermining the very cause he is so deeply passionate about.

My sense is that Derek, and likely a few others in the room, do not value the concept of psychological safety because they don't fully understand what it is and, importantly, what it is not. Based on a few remarks he has made in the past, I believe that Derek thinks of psychological safety as "being nice to each other," avoiding conflict, or even shielding ourselves from accountability. If that's how he understands the concept, no wonder he can't get on board with the idea! If that's what psychological safety meant, we wouldn't like it either.

What Psychological Safety Is Not

Although an increase in psychological safety usually makes the dynamics of a group feel warmer, more open, and less intimidating, this is not a "soft" idea in any way. Yet it is often misunderstood as a touchy-feely concept that's nice to consider, but not essential. In a 2021 *Forbes* article, CEO and author Timothy Clark dispels this myth well by summarizing what psychological safety is not[8]:

- A shield from accountability
- Niceness
- Coddling
- Consensus decision-making
- Unearned autonomy
- Political correctness

When we can dispel these myths in our mind, we become more open to seeing the relationship between psychological safety, an intentional culture, and organizational effectiveness. As Amy Edmondson reminds us, "Psychological safety is not a nice to have; it's essential for unleashing talent and value."[9]

Looking Under the Hood

But just *how* does psychological safety unlock team potential? As the research on psychological safety evolves, we understand the answer to this question better. While many people are studying the concept, we find Timothy Clark's work on this topic particularly valuable. Clark's framework suggests that there are four different stages of psychological safety that build upon each other and are often progressively more difficult to achieve.[10] Each stage brings with it an additional degree of opportunity for more valuable individual contributions, more helpful group norms, better collective decision-making, and higher quality output by the team. These stages of psychological safety are built on the idea that humans have a universal set of needs and that each stage respects and honors a particular need. In a short summary, here are the four stages:

Stage 1: Inclusion Safety

While inclusion has thankfully become a bigger focus for many organizations in recent years, the concept is often considered too narrow. Inclusion efforts are often targeted at ensuring that people in typically marginalized or underprivileged groups (people of color, LGBTQ+ people, women in male-dominated environments, etc.) are heard, seen, valued, and able to contribute fully. While this focus on marginalized groups is essential, it's important to widen our mental horizons and remember that nearly everyone struggles with feeling excluded at certain times and in certain circumstances. Inclusion should not be considered just a component of formal diversity, equity, inclusion, and belonging (DEIB) initiatives, but rather a universal concern because it lies at the heart of learning, contributing, and challenging the status quo; in other words, it's at the heart of a thriving culture.

Inclusion safety is also foundational. It is the prerequisite for the next three stages of safety, each of which asks people to take on greater interpersonal and psychological risk. When individuals do not first experience a sense of belonging—when they are unsure whether they are accepted or wanted—it becomes far more difficult for them to speak up, learn openly, contribute meaningfully, or challenge existing ways of working. Without inclusion safety, progress through the later stages is slow, fragile, or stalled altogether.

Consider a new hire joining a team where everyone else has worked together for years. Even if the new team member shares the same demographics as the majority, they may still feel like an outsider. Small signals such as a lack of eye contact in meetings, inside jokes they don't understand, or colleagues who stick to their usual lunch group can quickly reinforce that sense of exclusion. The We Work of Inclusion safety means the team intentionally invites that new hire into conversations, seeks their input, and makes the effort to help them feel that they belong.

Stage 2: Learner Safety

Once people feel included, the next hurdle is whether it's safe to learn out loud—to ask questions, admit mistakes, or say, "I don't know." It's not about whether learning is possible in theory (most organizations theoretically value learning); it's about whether people believe they can engage in the messy process of learning without judgment or punishment. This stage is critical because, no matter what functional role your team inhabits, your most important job is to learn together quickly, at or faster than the rate of change.

Imagine a frontline employee in a technical role who is asked to learn a new software system. If they feel they must pretend to understand everything immediately, they may nod along in meetings but struggle in silence. By contrast, their Me Work would be to ask "basic" questions with humility and curiosity so they can learn faster and make fewer mistakes. Learner safety shows up when people model curiosity themselves, admitting what they don't know, asking questions of others, and treating mistakes as material for growth rather than reasons for blame. Learner safety also involves leaders and others with decision-making authority and influence to identify and remove any barriers that exist to learning.

Stage 3: Contributor Safety

When the right conditions exist, most people have an innate desire to contribute fully to their organization. But if they don't feel included or can't learn well, they will not be willing or able to turn this desire into reality. Contributor Safety is the stage where individuals feel invited and able to apply their skills, ideas, and energy to make a meaningful difference. It's no longer about asking for permission to join; it's about stepping forward to add value with confidence that their efforts will be welcomed.

Picture an engineer who sees a way to streamline a recurring process. If she believes the environment is psychologically safe, she'll be more likely to share her idea, knowing it will be acknowledged and appreciated, even if it is not ultimately used. In an environment she deems unsafe, she may keep quiet, fearing her suggestion will be judged poorly or dismissed. Contributor safety thrives when leaders are doing their We Work and actively invite input, recognize contributions, and clarify that good ideas are not only for those at the top. The message is: "We value what you think and can do. Please share it with us."

Stage 4: Challenger Safety

The final stage is the hardest to reach but also the most transformative: Challenger Safety. This is where people feel secure enough to question assumptions, push back on established practices, and suggest new ways of doing things, even if it challenges those in authority or might make others uncomfortable. Without this stage, organizations may maintain harmony on the surface but stagnate underneath.

Consider an employee who notices that a long-standing process creates unnecessary obstacles to getting work done efficiently. Raising the issue means calling into question the system, and possibly the people who designed it. If the employee feels the environment is safe enough, he can voice his concern without fear of retaliation, knowing his input will be treated as an opportunity to improve rather than as insubordination. At this stage, disagreement is reframed as a sign of engagement, and constructive dissent becomes a driver of innovation and progress. Me Work in Challenger Safety is developing the courage to speak truth with respect, even when it's uncomfortable. Most teams have a lot of We Work to do around Challenger Safety focused in large part on their communication patterns with each other. We'll explore this fully in Chapter 8.

The Love Hormone

If psychological safety is a *feeling* we have about the degree of interpersonal safety, what is the basis for our individual subjective assessments? Where does the feeling of interpersonal safety (or the opposite) come from? Answering this question requires a quick trip into the world of neuroscience.

Neurobiologically speaking, the *feeling* of the presence of psychological safety is the result of a physiological shift in our brain and body involving the amygdala and a hormone called oxytocin. You might have heard of oxytocin before. It's commonly known as "the love hormone." It plays a significant role in maternal bonding. But it surges in the body in many other situations, too: when someone shares something vulnerable with us; when we laugh authentically, sing, or dance with other people; when we express or receive genuine gratitude. Essentially, oxytocin is released when the brain assesses "it's safe here." As oxytocin is released, the amygdala quiets. This makes sense because the amygdala is the part of our brain that detects threats and triggers fear or arousal to help protect us from danger.

Our human brains are wired to assess our environment for threats. Eons ago, in primitive times, our brains were often assessing for threats like famine or attack by wild animals or other tribes. Although most of us fortunately don't have to face those threats anymore, our brains still actively assess our environment for other types of threats: to our ego, to our emotional well-being or sense of belonging, to our professional or financial security, even to our self-image. Our modern-day brains' assessments of threat or safety are largely based on cues we pick up from other people's communication, their body language, tone of voice, and choice of words. (This last point is so important, we dedicate the next chapter to communication.)

To understand the importance of these neurobiological shifts in how they relate to workplace culture and performance, you might think about this visual (see Figure 7.1).

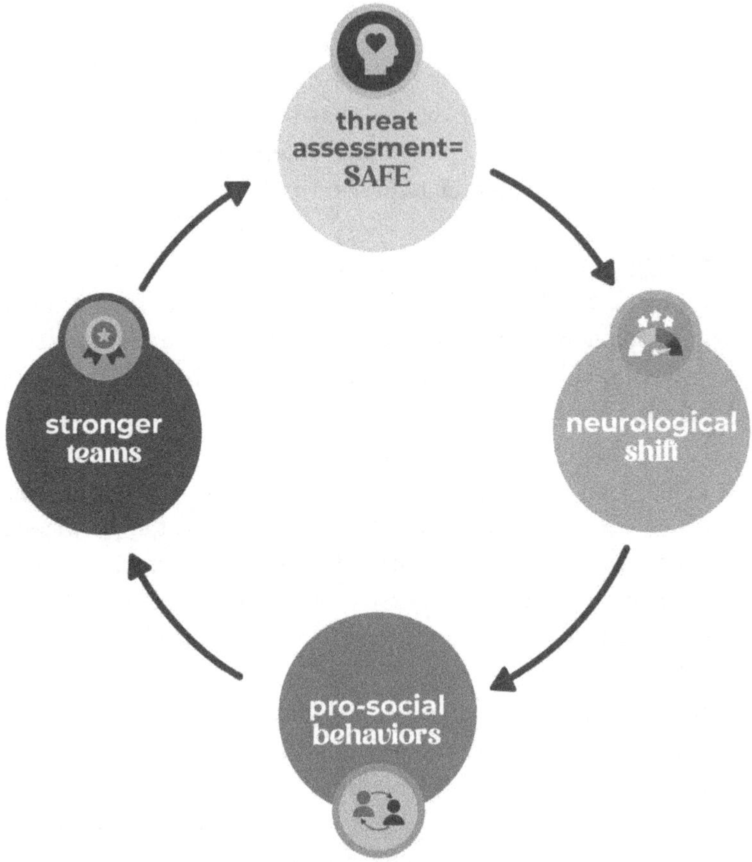

FIGURE 7.1 The psychological safety cycle.

In simplified terms, the cycle works like this:

- If our brain assesses a person or group as interpersonally safe, the amygdala quiets and we experience a surge of oxytocin.
- Oxytocin encourages "pro-social behaviors" such as remembering socially relevant information, expressing empathy, and collaborating more willingly.
- Over time, a group of people engaging in pro-social behaviors develop stronger bonds and, thus, stronger teams (both culturally and performance-wise).

- When our team is stronger as a result of these frequent pro-social behaviors, our brain more easily assesses it as "safe" and the cycle continues.

Over time, we create an upward spiral of perceived safety, helpful neurobiological states, and pro-social behaviors.

If the opposite conditions exist within and around us, a downward spiral is possible too. If we consciously or unconsciously assess our team as "unsafe," our amygdala stays on alert and produces fear and arousal. Oxytocin is less present or absent altogether. We engage less often in pro-social behaviors and are more likely to feel and be experienced by others as guarded, withdrawn, or reactive. Our team becomes interpersonally weak, and we begin to assess it, or certain members of it, as "unsafe." And the cycle continues.

What This Means for You

No matter where you sit in the organization, you influence the perceived degree of psychological safety in every group you are a part of. What you say and do—and how you say and do it—energetically changes the feeling in the room—and thus other's perception of what's safe, moment by moment. Even if you are not a formal leader with direct reports, you influence psychological safety for better or for worse by what you demonstrate, reward, and discourage.

If you are a formal leader, your influence is even greater because of your authority and positional power (the power that comes with your title). Not only do you need to pay attention to your *own* intentions and impact, you need to pay attention to the behavior of others on your team. The degree of perceived psychological safety can plummet on a team where just one person is chronically defensive or disrespectful to others, even if that person is not the formal leader. As cultural architect, your role is to ensure other people's undermining behaviors are addressed and that there is a high standard of accountability for psychological safety. You'll learn more about *how* to increase cultural accountability in Chapter 10.

Assess Yourself

There are many ways we can evaluate our own impact on psychological safety. This short assessment focuses on six broad influencers. As you learn about each, you'll be asked to rate how true a statement is for you. There are six statements total. As with every assessment we offer, the purpose of this is to increase self-awareness and inspire self-development. Although you may find this creates some discomfort for you, there is no need to feel bad about yourself if you score lower on any influencer. This a nonjudgmental look in the mirror that can help you see reality more clearly and be intentional about your Me Work and We Work.

The first time you complete this assessment, think about the team of people you work most closely with. Then, you're welcome to complete it again thinking about other groups you're a part of.

Influencer #1: Personal Energy

Have you noticed how some people seem to naturally "warm the air" when they enter a room? And other people seem to "cool the air"? That feeling you get from people the minute they enter a real or virtual room—that's energy.

Think about the people you know who warm up a room when they enter it. What do they do? They smile, make eye contact, and greet people directly. They might make their way to new people and proactively introduce themselves. They remember and say people's names. They take what feels like a genuine interest in others. They might be more prone to telling stories, using humor, listening well, and asking good questions. They emanate a blend of confidence and humility. In fancy terms, they engage in pro-social behaviors. In regular terms, they seem to lean into the human side of being human.

What do these warm energy people *not* typically do? They don't prioritize their phone or laptop over paying attention to the humans in the room. They don't sit off to the side by themselves and look disinterested or too busy. They don't say hello to only one person and skip greeting others. They don't make overly sarcastic or snide remarks. They don't gossip.

The first time I (Natalie) assessed myself on the energy influencer, I gave myself a high score. I have naturally high energy and try to bring optimism and connection into every room. But I've learned that not every moment calls for high energy or optimism. Once, I walked into a tense team conversation where people were frustrated and quiet. Wanting to lift the mood, I jumped in with enthusiasm and comments about how things could be worse. Instead of easing the tension, I could feel the room shut down. My energy landed as dismissive. It signaled that I wasn't fully understanding their frustration or making space for it. That moment taught me that "warming the air" isn't always about being social, energetic, or optimistic. Sometimes it's about grounding, softening, and matching the emotional energy in the room.

How does your personal energy affect the groups you're a part of?

Rate the following statement:

My personal energy warms the air and fosters openness and human connection.

Strongly Disagree | Disagree | Slightly Disagree | Slightly Agree | Agree | Strongly Agree

Influencer #2: Asking Versus Telling

Eugene Ionesco is credited with saying "It is not the answer that enlightens, but the question." We have found this to be deeply true. Powerful questions are an integral part of our work, from discovery through sustainability.[11] Well-timed, well-worded questions open up possibilities that definitive statements often do not—possibilities for deeper connection, transformative learning, self-development, interpersonal growth, problem-solving, understanding what matters, and developing critical thinking skills. On the other hand, too much telling tends to shift people into a resistant or self-protective mode, shutting down possibilities and connection.

Imagine your colleague shares a new idea for solving a chronic problem the team is facing. The idea is not fully flushed out but you don't initially like where it's going. Here are three examples of responses you might opt for:

- *I don't think that will work.*
- *Why would we do that?*
- *Can you tell me more about how that might work?*

Which one of those responses is most likely to foster a sense of inclusion, make it easier for the person to fully contribute their thoughts, and allow the team to learn quickly? Number three. While number two is technically a question, most people tend to feel at least mildly defensive when asked questions that begin with "Why," especially if they are asked with negative intent and/or a tone of voice that indicates dismissiveness or condescension. It's important to pay attention to your ratio of asking versus telling, and it's just as important to pay attention to the *intention* and *quality* of your questions.

Rate the following statement:

Through intentional listening and good questions, I draw people out instead of shut them down.

Influencer #3: Responding to Mistakes

Because human beings are fallible, mistakes are inevitable. If handled with intention, mistakes can be an avenue for learning, growth, and innovation. But most of us view mistakes as "bad"—moments, choices, or outcomes to be hidden from public view, especially if we fear serious disapproval or rejection. If you're not hearing about mistakes on your team, it doesn't mean they aren't happening. It just means people aren't admitting them, and that means the team is stripped of the opportunity to learn and they are more likely to be made again or spiral into something worse.

Think about a time someone brought you a mistake. How did you respond? Consider your words, tone, and body language. Were you curious and steady, or frustrated and sharp? Leaders and teammates who respond with curiosity, empathy, and problem-solving energy communicate that mistakes are a natural part of learning. Those who react with irritation, sarcasm, or blame teach people to hide, usually at the cost of inclusion, learning, and contribution.

Amy Edmondson's research suggests that how people respond *the moment* someone makes or shares a mistake often dictates whether that person will feel safe in the circumstances moving forward. If you realize your immediate response was unhelpful, you can certainly ask for a "re-do" and offer a different response. But it's important to pay attention to your *immediate* response.

Rate the following statement:

When mistakes occur—mine or others'—I respond in ways that preserve dignity, invite learning, and keep relationships intact.

○	○	○	○	○	○
Strongly Disagree	Disagree	Slightly Disagree	Slightly Agree	Agree	Strongly Agree

Influencer #4: Inviting and Managing Dissent

Most of us like the idea of open dialogue, until disagreement enters the room. Dissent can feel uncomfortable, even threatening. Yet healthy disagreement is often the birthplace of insight, innovation, and better decisions. Inviting dissent means signaling that different perspectives are not only welcome, but necessary. Managing dissent means helping those perspectives surface productively, so disagreement strengthens rather than fracture the group. (More on this in Chapter 9, which is all about navigating conflict.)

Imagine you're in a meeting where everyone seems to agree quickly on a plan. One team member hesitates, clearly unsure. You could move on and preserve harmony, or pause and say, "I noticed you looked uncertain. What's your take?" That small invitation can change everything. You've opened the door to deeper thinking, surfaced hidden concerns, and modeled that difference is valued. Inviting dissent doesn't mean you have to agree with every viewpoint. It means you respect the courage it takes to voice one, and you help channel that courage toward better collective outcomes.

Rate the following statement:

I create space for differing views and help turn disagreement into dialogue, not division.

○	○	○	○	○	○
Strongly Disagree	Disagree	Slightly Disagree	Slightly Agree	Agree	Strongly Agree

Influencer #5: Speaking Candidly

When we speak candidly, we tell others what is true for us, while being clear, kind, and without unnecessary delay. It takes courage to speak up when something is off, when a decision feels misaligned, or when silence would be easier. But withholding candor often costs more over time: misunderstandings deepen, problems linger, and trust erodes. (More on this in Chapter 8, which is all about communication, including candor.)

Think of a time you needed to say something hard to someone. Maybe you softened it so much the message got lost or avoided it altogether. What might have happened if you'd named the truth with care and clarity instead? Or perhaps the opposite is true for you: you're very comfortable speaking directly but you sometimes do so without enough attention to care and respect. Candor paired with compassion signals maturity and trustworthiness. It tells people you care enough about them and the team to say what needs to be said in a way that people will be most likely to receive with minimal defensiveness.

Rate the following statement:

I communicate the truth with clarity and care, even when the conversation feels uncomfortable.

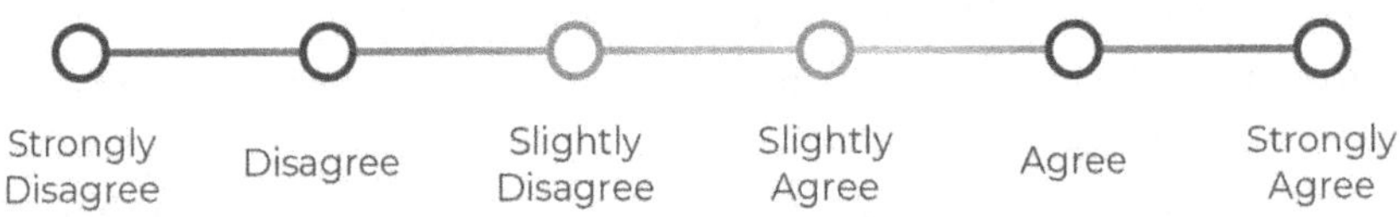

Influencer #6: Receiving Feedback

Both giving and receiving feedback can feel vulnerable, and both require courage. Many of us instinctively brace when someone says, "Can I give you some feedback?" But feedback, especially when we can receive it openly, is one of the fastest ways to grow. The key is to listen past our initial defensiveness and look for the learning inside the message.

Picture yourself getting feedback that stings a little. You can shut down, argue, or withdraw. Or you can breathe, thank the person, and ask a question or two to understand more. That moment of composure builds trust and models the learning mindset you want in others. Even if you don't agree with the feedback, it's important that you demonstrate the ability to receive it well so that others experience you as "safe" in this regard.

Rate the following statement:

I welcome feedback as valuable input for my growth and respond with gratitude and curiosity instead of judgment and defensiveness.

Strongly Disagree	Disagree	Slightly Disagree	Slightly Agree	Agree	Strongly Agree
○	○	○	○	○	○

What to Do from Here

Now what? Let's think about these psychological safety influencers through the lens of Me Work and We Work. Here are a few practical strategies for taking your learning from this chapter and translating it into the type of Me Work and We Work that fundamentally evolves culture.

Me Work

- **Identify your strongest influencer.** Notice what you already do well. Your natural strengths are part of how you build psychological safety around you. Be intentional about continuing to use that strength more often.
- **Choose one development opportunity.** Look at your lowest-rated influencer and make a small, specific commitment to grow in that area for a month (for example, "Ask one genuine question before offering an opinion in meetings").
- **Seek perspective.** Ask a trusted colleague or friend for feedback on how they experience you in one or two of these influencers. Listen with curiosity, not defensiveness.

We Work

- **Use the assessment as a team conversation tool.** Have team members take it individually, then discuss patterns or insights together. Focus on what would most strengthen the team's sense of safety and trust.

- **Model and invite growth.** Share your own self-assessment results—or one area you're working on—with your team. This signals humility and normalizes development.
- **Integrate the language.** Use these influencers in regular check-ins, debriefs, and performance conversations. The more they're named and discussed, the more they shape how the group works together.

The Most Important Thing to Know

Just in case we haven't made this explicitly clear, the reason we're spending so much time in this book on the concept of psychological safety is because it's the *most essential ingredient* in designing and nurturing an intentional, values-based culture where people have the greatest chance of thriving. In the following chapters, we'll talk about other essential ingredients: effective communication, navigating conflict, accountability, and defining desired culture. It's important to understand the cyclical relationship here:

- When we focus on increasing psychological safety, we usually end up naturally communicating more effectively, navigating conflict more productively, and creating greater accountability.
- And, interestingly, when we get better at these important skillsets, it often *results in* an increase in psychological safety.

It's all important, but if you're wondering, "Where do I start?" psychological safety is the answer.

One final point is important here: the vulnerability required to experience psychological safety is not the same for everyone. The level of risk people feel and the potential consequences they weigh can vary significantly depending on context, role, and identity. For example, speaking up may feel very different if you are the only woman on an all-male engineering team, the only person of color in a work group, or someone with less positional power. What feels like a small interpersonal risk to one person may feel consequential to another. As we focus on psychological safety, we must do so keeping this reality in mind.

8 Communication

Seth

I (Natalie) am meeting with an IT leader about tension brewing inside one of his teams that stems from the communication style of the team leader, Seth. He shares an example:

> "Last week, I heard one of his employees expressing frustration about a colleague who wasn't pulling their weight. I heard Seth say something to the effect of *'Just do your job and don't worry about it.'* Honestly, it's not the first time I've heard him talk to people that way."

He paused. "Technically, he's sharp. He is smart and efficient. But the way he communicates is shutting people down and that's starting to affect the team."

Our IT leader is worried for good reason. When a leader's communication style becomes a source of stress, psychological safety erodes, initiative disappears, and people start protecting themselves instead of contributing their best.

The Nearly Universal Me Work

If you think back to the six psychological safety influencers we highlighted in the last chapter (personal energy, asking versus telling, mistakes, dissent, speaking candidly, receiving truth), you'll see they all have one thing in common: communication. Of course they do! Communication is the primary way human beings interact, and we are consciously or unconsciously communicating messages all day long, every day.

Seth is certainly not alone in his need for Me Work on communication. It's no exaggeration to say that *most of* us have Me Work to do related to communication if we want to fulfill our own potential, help others fulfill theirs, lead intentional cultures, and catalyze high performance. This chapter offers concrete ideas, practical strategies, and tools you can use to strengthen and fine-tune communication patterns.

Why Is It So Hard to Communicate Well?

Even in the best of scenarios, face-to-face in the same room with someone we know well, speaking the same language, human communication is complex. Although we communicate verbally and nonverbally all day long and have been doing so since birth, it remains surprisingly difficult to do it effectively. Why is that? There are many reasons, but here's a short list:

- We send messages through our own subjective lens, and others receive them through theirs. One person expresses her perspective; the other interprets something different.
- Our verbal and nonverbal communication is shaped by major factors like knowledge, past experience, age, gender, cultural norms, and ethnicity that can result in differences, gaps, and misunderstandings.
- It's also influenced by our relationship with the other person: how safe they feel to us, how long we've known them, and the assumptions we make about them.
- Smaller factors can interfere with effective communication as well, such as technology distractions, our mood, physical sensations like pain or hunger, or even differences in how we interpret specific words or facial expressions.

- The more people involved, say, in a large meeting, the more complex the exchange becomes, and the greater the chance for misunderstanding.

All of these elements shape the story we tell ourselves about what's happening and why. Over time, these stories become the narratives we hold about people, teams, and situations. The narratives feel true even when they are incomplete or inaccurate. Unless we pause to examine them, these narratives will drive our communication, reactions, relationships, and ultimately our culture.

Communication Traps

As we are navigating this field of communication land mines, we often fall into common traps. We think of these traps as "softer" behaviors and "harder" behaviors. Softer doesn't mean better or less problematic; just that they tend to be experienced by others as less edgy, but they still undermine communication and create disconnection with other people.

As you read the list of softer and harder communication traps, check the ones you tend to fall into. You might end up with lots of checks, or only just a few. As you know by now, the purpose of self-assessment is not to berate ourselves and feel guilty; it's to become more self-aware and intentional about what we choose to start, stop, or continue doing as we're leading our own CultureJourney.

"Softer" Behaviors	"Harder" Behaviors
☐ Procrastinate excessively	☐ Talk "at" people without listening enough or asking questions
☐ Avoid tough conversations altogether	☐ Speak your truth without empathy or compassion ("brutal honesty")
☐ Sugar coat	☐ Deliver information when the receiver is not expecting it or may not be able to receive it well (i.e., when they are deeply involved in something else or highly stressed)
☐ Bury the main point in too many other words	☐ React defensively when hearing information that makes you uncomfortable
☐ Apologize unnecessarily	
☐ Use filler words excessively (i.e., "like," "ah," "um," "so")	
☐ Fail to prepare adequately (mentally or emotionally) for the conversation so you are unclear or disorganized	

A Deeper Dive

As you review the list of communication traps, what comes up for you? Do you lean toward softer behaviors, harder behaviors, or a mix? Did you just identify possible Me Work for yourself or validate Me Work you already knew you needed to do?

Here's a key point: Knowing *what* unhelpful behaviors we tend toward (around communication or anything else) is valuable. But knowing *why* you do them is even more valuable.

When we facilitate communication training, we often ask participants to explore the deeper reasons behind their tendencies. We hear all sorts of responses, like:

- "I worry that if I get to the point too quickly, I'll come across as [fill in the blank: cold, rude, too direct, too task-focused]."
- "I'm afraid I'll upset the other person."
- "Sometimes I just get on a roll and forget to pause, ask questions, or listen."
- "I prefer directness and wish I didn't have to spend so much time on 'niceties'."
- "I'm not even sure why I do this. I've never really thought about it."

Let's say you relate with the first example. You tend to sugar coat messages instead of speaking directly because you're concerned you'll come across as cold or "bossy" if you simply say what you mean. If you peel pack your "why" a few layers more, you might discover more important information, such as:

- If this person were to perceive you as cold or bossy, they might disapprove of you or not like you as much
- If they disapproved or didn't like you, the quality of your relationship might deteriorate
- You might feel worried, regret, or loneliness if this happened, or experience other negative consequences because of the deterioration of the relationship

By asking *why* we do what we do, we often reveal the real challenge beneath the surface. In this common example, you could benefit from being more direct. But the issue isn't just about your words. It's about exploring and addressing your concern that honesty might damage your relationships. You might need to check old assumptions, rewrite internal narratives, learn how to communicate both directly *and* with care, and navigate the discomfort of other people's discomfort. This is all important Me Work that lies at the heart of this seemingly simple change from sugar coating to candor. If we're not aware of the deeper Me Work that exists under an inner operating system update we want to make, we're unlikely to successfully make the update.

Take a few moments now to reflect on one or two of the communication traps you just identified. Think more deeply about this than you normally might. Peel back the layers a bit.

Communication trap #1: ______________________________

I do this because . . .

And by doing this, I'm trying to avoid or control . . .

Communication trap #2: ______________________________

I do this because . . .

And by doing this, I'm trying to avoid or control . . .

Let's move now to tools, strategies, and practices that can help you avoid these traps and update your inner operating system, so you develop a more effective communication style that builds psychological safety and influences group norms.

It's All About Your Energy

The Vidl Work team has been facilitating trainings and conversations about communication for years. In the past, we would often teach important concepts like empathy, listening, inquiry, and candor and then—at the very end of the session—discuss "reducing defensiveness." At some point, we realized that we were sharing ideas in the wrong order and thinking too narrowly about the concept of defensiveness. "Reducing defensiveness" is a part of a broader need to *regulate our own personal energy*. And it's not an afterthought to save for the end of a skill-building session on communication: it's the starting point.

Think about yourself when you are tired, anxious, hungry, overwhelmed, angry, taxed, or drained. If you're like most people, these energetic states are not the conditions from which you demonstrate the best version of yourself. In these states, we're more likely to interrupt people, react defensively, use unhelpful words, focus on being right, dismiss people's ideas, or shut down. It's just *hard* to be present or intentional when our energy is out of whack. We inadvertently demonstrate unhelpful behaviors and potentially undermine psychological safety. But when we're well-rested, calm, centered, energized, and focused, *that's when we can tap into our own best self*.

When we get better at recognizing and regulating our physical, mental, emotional, and spiritual energy in the moment, we are more likely to be able to express empathy, listen well, ask good questions, and speak courageously. This is one of the most important reasons we include such a big focus on energy in the Me Work and We Work assessments. Because regulating our energy is the first step in effective communication, which is essential for psychological safety, changing cultural norms, and attending to system issues.

Practice #1: Regulate Emotional Reactivity

Since the experience of communication-blockers like reactivity or defensiveness happen primarily in the body, we need to get better at noticing what they feel like in our body and then using in-the-moment practices to regulate our nervous system. We often help people do this work with a simple activity.

First, think about the last time you were in conversation and you felt defensive. Bring that situation to life in writing with just a few sentences here.

Now, think about what was happening in your *body* at that moment. How did you feel physically—or what did you do? Check all that apply:

- ☐ Flushed/red skin
- ☐ Clenched jaw
- ☐ Clenched fists
- ☐ Heart rate increased
- ☐ Clenching sensation in my chest
- ☐ Clenching sensation in my throat
- ☐ Changes in my breathing
- ☐ Knots in my stomach
- ☐ Crossed my arms
- ☐ Strong impulse to interrupt
- ☐ Strong desire to leave the situation
- ☐ Leaned or moved back
- ☐ Leaned or moved toward

Once you know your signs of reactivity or defensiveness, you can begin to be on the lookout for them and see them as "red flags" signaling that something within you needs attention. When you notice one or more of these red flags arise, what can you do to stay calm, present, and open for the conversation? Here are a few ideas. Place a mark by any that you can visualize yourself doing:

- ☐ Breathe deeply and slowly
- ☐ Notice the grounding sensation of my feet on the floor
- ☐ Focus on listening
- ☐ Ask questions to understand
- ☐ Assume the other person has positive intentions toward me
- ☐ Say helpful words to myself (i.e., "The most important thing right now is to stay calm" or simply "Relax")
- ☐ Offer gratitude to the person for their input, feedback, or perspectives
- ☐ Acknowledge out loud that I'm feeling defensive and ask for time before responding

In addition to these general practices, we often share two specific tools that are helpful in identifying, regulating, and recovering emotional energy: the emotional energy quadrants and The Line. You can find a one-page worksheet on each of these tools in the resource section of our website. (See the callout box at the end of this chapter.)

Communication Commitment #1: Reducing Reactivity and Defensiveness

When I noticing I'm feeling reactive or defensive, I commit to . . .

Practice #2: Lean into Empathy

Think of a time when you were in conversation with another person and felt that they really *got you* and they truly understood what you were feeling. You were left *feeling felt*. In that moment, you were probably experiencing empathy from another person.

Empathy is the ability to sit with someone else's emotions and allow them to exist in a safe space, without judgment, fixing, or dismissal. It doesn't require that you fully understand what the other person is feeling (which is good, because that's not always possible) or that you've experienced the same thing yourself. What it does require is that you listen for the other person's experience and believe that what they're experiencing is real for them, even if you have had a different experience.

Our ability to experience and express empathy has real-life implications at home and at work. It's a foundational element that makes *all* communication better; it doesn't need to be reserved only for when another person is clearly in struggle. Whether you're sharing new information with your team, offering difficult feedback to a peer, learning about a mistake, or receiving challenging news yourself, empathy helps. Sometimes, it's all that's needed. Other times, it provides the foundation upon which you can build with curiosity, candor, or accountability. Fortunately, if empathy doesn't come naturally to you, it's a skill you can develop with awareness and practice.

Many of us don't demonstrate empathy well, not because we don't care, but because we don't really know what it is, haven't been taught, confuse it with other things, or simply haven't practiced enough. Here's what empathy is *not*:

- Judging
- Minimizing
- Being disappointed in
- Comparing or competing
- Giving unsolicited advice
- Trying to solve another person's problem

Let's look at a practical example.

Shanna

Shanna supervises a small team in the facilities department. One of her employees, Marcus, has been missing deadlines and turning in incomplete work. Shanna knows she needs to address the issue, but she also knows Marcus has been under unusual personal stress.

Before their meeting, Shanna takes a moment to center herself. She reminds herself that the goal isn't to *win* the conversation; it's to understand and help Marcus succeed. When they sit down, she begins with curiosity:

> "Marcus, I've noticed you've been missing deadlines lately, which isn't like you. I wanted to check in, how are things going for you right now?"

As Marcus explains what's been going on, Shanna listens fully. She doesn't interrupt, rush to fix, or downplay what he's saying. She acknowledges his situation and reflects back what she's heard before moving to next steps. The tone of the conversation shifts from defensive to collaborative. Shanna helps Marcus feel heard and supported, which makes it far more likely that the accountability part of the discussion that happens next will go well.

Empathy Can Be Hard!

As essential a building block as it is, empathy is also *really hard* sometimes. It's typically more difficult for us to generate empathy when we're multitasking, distracted, working with a dysregulated nervous system, or simply not in the mood (thus the importance of energy management). It can also be hard to generate empathy for certain people, especially those who trigger us emotionally, who we don't like, or who we disagree with.

Here are a few ideas when you're finding it difficult to generate empathy:

- Think of a time when you may have been in a similar situation or feeling something similar to what this person is feeling. How would you like to have been treated in that moment?
- Mentally connect with something you value about this person, even if it's a seemingly small attribute or you have to dig deep to find it.
- Assume best intent. Consider that everyone is doing the best they can in the moment, even if that "best" doesn't feel comfortable or valuable to you right now. Remember that there have been times when you were doing your best and other people may not have thought so.
- Connect with the idea that this person is someone's child. If this were a child you loved, what feelings would naturally arise? How would you show up for them?
- Bring this idea to the forefront of your mind and even say it to yourself: *whatever else I am wanting to happen in this conversation, empathy will increase the chances of it happening.*

Communication Commitment #2: Empathy

When I notice I'm having a hard time generating empathy, I commit to . . .

Practice #3: Listen with Helpful Intentions

If there were a list of underappreciated culture-building skills, intentional listening would be near the top. Learning to listen deeply and intently to others is a true game changer. Yet most of us don't listen well, especially when we're distracted or defensive. Stephen Covey famously said, "Most of us don't listen with the intent to understand; we listen with the intent to reply." We've found this to be true in our own lives and in our work with hundreds of clients.

Even when we're calm and centered, many obstacles get in the way of listening: our own internal chatter, impulsive reactions, and the endless interruptions and distractions from technology and other people. One significant obstacle is that we often enter conversations with an unconscious agenda that limits potential. Unconscious, unhelpful intentions include:

- Getting the conversation over quickly
- Making sure the other person likes or approves of us
- Proving that we're smart or right
- Solving the other person's problem (even when they haven't asked for help or we don't yet understand what the actual problem is)

When we enter a conversation with these intentions, we're unlikely to listen well. We may even undermine psychological safety, create *dis*connection, or model behaviors we wouldn't want to see from other people.

Instead, what if we entered more conversations with conscious intentions that are helpful? Think of a recent conversation that didn't go as well as you hoped, one that felt unfulfilling, unnecessarily tense, or unproductive. Imagine how the tone, flow, and outcome might have changed if you had decided to listen with one or more of these intentions:

- To remain calm and curious
- To be fully present
- To stay open-minded
- To learn something new
- To understand better

- To sit with discomfort without reacting to it
- To get to the heart of what matters

Let's revisit the story of Seth from the beginning of this chapter and imagine a different outcome. What if, after his employee shared her concerns about another employee "slacking," Seth had been able to regulate his own nervous system, reduce reactivity, and increase his intentionality? He might have been better able to access empathy and listen with true intention to both what she was saying and what was "between" the words.

Had he done so, he might have chosen any number of helpful responses, such as:

- Recognize that he was in an agitated state and unable to respond thoughtfully. Acknowledge this out loud to his employee and ask for time to reflect, then commit to reconnecting later in the day so he could bring his best self to the conversation.
- Take a few slow, deep breaths as she spoke to regulate his nervous system, choosing to listen with intention and get to the heart of what matters. Let her speak fully, then say, "I hear you. What feels most important to you about this?"
- Offer himself a quiet reminder to "Stay present right now" and choose to listen to understand. After she finished, say, "I've heard you talk about this before, but I haven't fully understood the problem. Can you say more about how this is impacting you and the team?"

By regulating his energy, connecting with empathy, and listening with helpful intentions, Seth would have demonstrated a valuable energy and connection choice for Lisa. Seth's colleague may have left feeling *rewarded* for expressing vulnerable concern rather than discouraged. Both would have gained deeper insight into a team dynamic needing attention, empowering them to respond thoughtfully.

While this single moment would have been improved through more effective communication, imagine the larger impact on culture and daily work life if the same approach were multiplied across hundreds or thousands of conversations over time.

Communication Commitment #3: Listening with Intention

What often gets in the way of me listening with helpful intentions is . . .

When I notice this happening, I will . . ..

Practice #4: Ask Powerful Questions

As a leader, you have several overarching objectives, almost no matter what the situation or circumstance:

- To understand reality as clearly as you can
- To elicit your team member's best thinking
- To help your team members develop good judgment and effective decision-making

When you and your team can identify what really matters, what needs to be done, and how to act most effectively, you will spend less time managing other people's work and less energy dealing with drama and dysfunction.

But here's the tricky thing: many people are operating with ideas about how to influence and develop others that do not align with how human beings actually grow and change. This is especially true for older leaders who "grew up" in workplaces rooted in command-and-control hierarchies where positional power was used to make all the decisions and tell people what to do. The reality is that too much telling shuts people down, reduces intrinsic motivation and engagement, increases resistance and resentment, and strips people of the opportunity to develop their own critical thinking skills. This is not a recipe for success when it comes to workplace culture or organizational performance.

Eugene Ionesco's quote is worth repeating here: "It's not the answer that enlightens, but the question." If you choose to practice incorporating more and better questions into your communication style, we guarantee you'll notice a difference in the quality of the conversation and the ensuing outcomes.

But what questions to ask? And when?

Not All Questions Are Created Equal

Not all questions are equally valuable because different types of questions activate different parts of the brain. "Why" questions often trigger the brain's threat response, prompting defensiveness and rationalization rather than curiosity or problem-solving. The limbic system, which is largely responsible for emotional reactions, can take over, making people feel judged or pressured to justify themselves. In other words, "Why" questions often inadvertently elicit defensiveness. In contrast, questions that start with "What" or "How" engage the prefrontal cortex, the brain's center for reasoning, creativity, and reflection. These questions invite exploration and ownership, leading to more open, productive thinking and dialogue.

Also, different *scenarios* benefit from different types of questions. When helping our direct report figure out how to solve a problem, we might ask, "What options have you considered?" When we want to ensure we understand why someone is telling us something, we might ask, "What feels most important to you about this?" There are literally hundreds of powerful questions we could choose from. But you don't need to memorize hundreds of questions to become better at helpful inquiry; you just need to try out different questions, notice their impact, pay attention to which work best, and get in the habit of using your own personal library of questions on a more regular basis.

Identify Your Favorites

Read the following list of questions and place a mark by any you can imagine yourself using. Or, if you like the spirit of a question but would say it differently, rewrite it in your own words. If you think of other questions not listed, add them here.

To be sure you are receiving the message as intended:

- ☐ What I think I'm hearing is [BRIEF RECAP]. Did I get that right?
- ☐ Could you say that again or expand on what you're saying?
- ☐ What feels important about what you are telling me?
- ☐ Other: ____

To clarify priorities for a conversation or meeting:

- ☐ What would you like to get out of today's conversation?
- ☐ What would you like to focus on today?
- ☐ Given the time we have together, what's most important to you?
- ☐ Today, I'd like to make sure we cover [xxx] . . . What are your priorities?
- ☐ Where should we begin?
- ☐ Other: ____

To elicit best thinking about a problem or challenge:

- ☐ What stands out to you as important about this?
- ☐ What assumptions are we making that need further investigation?
- ☐ What else could be going on here?
- ☐ What's working well? What's valuable that we can build on?
- ☐ Where was there friction? What needs to be different?
- ☐ What are your ideas for change or a better solution?
- ☐ What can you do that would be helpful?
- ☐ What support do you need from me, the team, or elsewhere?
- ☐ Other: ____

During or after giving someone else feedback:

- ☐ What are your reactions to what I've said?
- ☐ I've offered my perspectives. What are yours?
- ☐ What do you see as the challenges or obstacles to improving this?
- ☐ What else do I need to know?
- ☐ What support do you need?
- ☐ Other: ____

To ask as or after you are receiving feedback from another person:

- ☐ What impact has this had on you or the team?
- ☐ What else would you like to share with me that you haven't yet?
- ☐ What would it look like if things were different or better?
- ☐ What are you needing from me, the team, or elsewhere?
- ☐ What are your suggestions on how we move forward?
- ☐ Can you say more?
- ☐ Other: ______________________________

Make This Easy

When we talk about this with clients, people are usually receptive to the idea that inquiry is more powerful than telling and even eager to practice asking more and better questions. But they often also express concern that they won't *remember* what questions they might ask in the moment. That's normal. If we're not in the practice of using inquiry more often in our conversations—which most people aren't—we'll need to give ourselves grace as we practice. And we need to make it easier for ourselves to get good at this. One simple way to make it easier is to download the list of Powerful Questions from our website (see the callout box at the end of this chapter) and then keep that list with you in the places you'll need it.

Communication Commitment #4: Ask Powerful Questions

My most important commitment around using inquiry is . . .

Practice #5: Speak Candidly

After years of working with thousands of people across an incredible range of teams and organizations, we've discovered something simple but profound: much of the friction, confusion, and underperformance that shows up at work could be reduced or even eliminated if people became more skilled and confident in speaking candidly and listening to others' truths without defensiveness. When spoken with genuine care and received with openness, truth is one of the most powerful ingredients in creating and sustaining a thriving culture. Yet candor often feels risky. It takes courage, commitment, and practice and most of us aren't naturally good at it.

Immanuel

I (Rebecca) am in a coaching session with Immanuel. He's sharing frustrations about his boss, Laura. Generally, he likes working with her, but lately she's made several decisions that impact his team without consulting him first.

"She's done this a few times, and I don't understand why," he says. "Does she not think I'm capable of making these decisions? It undermines my authority and confuses the team."

I've heard this before, so I ask whether he's talked with Laura about it.

"No," he admits. "I've thought about it, but I'm not sure I should."

We explore his hesitation: *What might happen if he shared his concerns directly? What's holding him back?*

Immanuel realizes he's avoiding the conversation for a few key reasons:

- He's unsure he can express himself with the confidence, clarity, and care he wants to convey.
- He fears Laura will be upset, possibly hurt, embarrassed, or defensive.
- If she reacts emotionally, he worries he won't know how to handle it.

In trying to protect himself from awkwardness or guilt and to preserve their relationship Immanuel stays silent. Ironically, his silence is eroding the very relationship he's trying to protect. He finds himself irritated, avoiding her, and trusting her less.

The Cost of Withholding

Immanuel's story is incredibly common. Most of us withhold more than we reveal: with peers, direct reports, family members, and even close friends. We hold back even more with people in positions of power, like our boss or other authority figures. Withholding is human and predictable. But it's costly.

In *The 15 Commitments of a Conscious Leader,*[1] Jim Dethmer, Diana Chapman, and Kaley Warner Klemp define a *withhold* as anything you've experienced three or more times (a thought, feeling, assumption, or even a bodily sensation) but haven't shared. They outline the costs of withholding:

- **Withholding drains energy.** Think about the last time you nodded in false agreement during a meeting or smiled when you were unsettled inside. Pretending requires effort. Over time, it's exhausting. Energy that could fuel presence, connection, and creativity gets trapped in concealment.
- **We lose sight of reality.** When Immanuel withholds his perspective, Laura can't see the full picture, and neither can he. Instead, he fills in the blanks with assumptions and reacts to his own stories. If he were to share his truth with care and curiosity and Laura received it well, they'd both gain a clearer view of reality and could move forward with greater understanding.
- **Relationships suffer.** When we conceal what feels true, we subtly distance ourselves from the other person. Over time, this gap widens. We begin to project more negative assumptions ("If I can't trust Jacob with this, maybe I can't trust him at all"), and our guardedness creates even more separation.

If you recall from earlier chapters our focus on the three important elements of energy, connection, and courage, you can probably begin to see how problematic chronic withholding is when our aim is to design and nurture an intentional culture.

Revealing Effectively

Here's an important distinction: speaking candidly is not the same thing as "brutal honesty." While operating in the realm of honesty can feel unusual, uncomfortable, and even painful at times, culture work does not require anything purposefully "brutal." If we choose to practice revealing more often, it does *not* mean we:

- give ourselves permission to say whatever thought or sensation pops into our head, whenever we feel like it, regardless of the circumstances
- express all unexamined thoughts or feelings right as the impulse arises
- right away say what we think the other person "needs to hear" so we can get things off our chest
- position our thoughts and feelings to others as a universal truth or "right"

What it *does* mean is that we:

- Pay attention to our thoughts, feelings, and bodily sensations and view them as valuable information that can help us more fully understand our own experience (albeit often after a bit of examination about the actual meaning of our thoughts, feelings, and sensations)
- Reveal more of what is true for us more of the time. And, importantly, do so with the recognition that what is "true" for us right now may evolve over time as we gain more information, shift our perspective, or regulate our own nervous system
- Share what is true for us in a particular way: openly, honestly, and *with care*
- Speak intentionally in the spirit of growth, development, trust, connection, and seeing reality clearly
- Remember that effective candor is a two-way street, so we practice *receiving* other people's current truths with the same degree of openness we want from them

If we carry this understanding into the practice of revealing more often, our practice will likely be more fruitful. It will not by any means go perfectly all the time. We'll still have our fair share of mess-ups, uncomfortable moments, and conversations that did not go as we intended. But that's okay. We are not striving for perfection but that is unattainable. We're aiming for progress.

Speaking Unarguably

When I (Rebecca) first heard the phrase "speaking unarguably," I felt a tinge of resistance to the idea. It felt to me as if this was a poorly disguised way of saying "speak so that other people can't argue with me so that I can be right." But I now understand that "speaking unarguably" simply means using language that would be difficult for others to argue with in good faith because it's about *my experience.*

When I use unarguable language, I do so with full awareness that other people have different experiences, thoughts, feelings, and sensations about the very same situation. I share not to prove a point or to be right, but to be known and help reality be seen more clearly. Conversely, when I use arguable language, I prime the situation for unnecessary drama and unhealthy debate.

Here are some examples of arguable versus unarguable language.

Arguable	Unarguable
We should not hire this person. They are not right for this role.	**I have been thinking** for a few days that this candidate may not be right for this role. **I'm concerned that** if we hire them . . .
You don't trust me.	**The story I'm telling myself** is that you don't trust me to lead my team well. I want to check this story out with you. Can you share your perspectives with me?
This project is not a good fit for you.	**I often experience anxiety** when you and I talk about this project together. **My sense** is that it is not going as well as it could be and **I'm wondering** whether this project is the right fit. Can we talk about this?
These meetings would be more effective if people stopped highjacking the conversation.	**I notice my energy drops** whenever our attempt to resolve issues takes longer than I think it should. **I believe** I see some of the challenges we're having and would like to talk about this with the group to make our meetings more effective.

But It Feels Risky!

It does. Speaking candidly always carries some degree of vulnerability, especially in environments where we haven't tested candor yet, where trust is low or where speaking up has led to negative consequences. On a human level, candor asks us to risk something essential: belonging. Our nervous systems are wired to protect connection because, for most of human history, belonging to the group meant survival. When we tell the truth, especially one that might disrupt comfort, challenge authority, or expose emotion we fear being misunderstood, dismissed, or excluded. The brain and body read that possibility as danger, even when the threat is social rather than physical.

One particular reason we avoid candor (often without even consciously knowing it) is that many of us are deeply concerned about what will happen if the person we're speaking with becomes upset. Immanuel, for example, was concerned that Laura might tear up if he offered her his truthful perspective, and he did not feel equipped to "handle" that. Another client we worked with realized she was worried about giving tough feedback to one of her team members for fear he would get visibly angry and "storm out" of the room.

Candor also feels risky because of the systems we work within. Many workplaces often unintentionally reward politeness, compliance, and productivity over curiosity, dissent, and reflection. Power hierarchies can make some voices safer than others. Unspoken rules ("Don't question your boss," "Don't make waves," "Stay positive") subtly teach us that harmony is more important than honesty. Over time, those cultural signals shape behavior. People learn to stay quiet, to smooth over tension, to edit themselves. The result is a kind of organizational armor that protects individuals but weakens the team because truth, trust, and innovation can't fully circulate through a guarded system.

Recognizing these dynamics doesn't make the risk disappear, but it helps us see that the discomfort of candor isn't a personal flaw; it's part of being human in a system that often prioritizes comfort over truth. Once we understand that, we can start to make new choices in the form of small, deliberate acts of courage that strengthen both our personal integrity and the relational fabric around us.

Practice

Speaking candidly becomes easier when we see it not as a single act of bravery, but as an ongoing practice. Here are a few ways to begin or deepen that practice:

- **Start with self-honesty.** Before you speak, check in with yourself: What feels true for me right now? What am I thinking or feeling, and what do I want to create by sharing it? Is now the right time? Am I in the right internal state to share it unarguably?

- **Attend to your body.** Breathe, ground, and regulate before speaking. When your nervous system feels safe, your words carry both clarity and calm.
- **Start small and safe.** Practice candor in lower-stakes situations first. Share a mild truth with someone who feels more psychologically safe, observe how it lands, and notice what you learn about yourself and others.
- **Anchor in care and curiosity.** Speak not to win or prove, but to connect and understand. Genuine curiosity transforms even hard truths into openings rather than attacks.
- **Name your intention.** Begin by sharing why you want to reveal; for example, you might say, "I value our working relationship, and I want to check in with you on a story I'm telling myself to understand your perspective on it."
- **Use unarguable language.** Describe your thoughts, feelings, and sensations rather than making claims about the other person's motives or character. ("I notice I feel uneasy when decisions happen without my input.")
- **Welcome the response.** Remember that others have their own truths. Stay open to what comes back not as a verdict, but as data for mutual understanding.
- **Normalize emotions.** If someone expresses emotion about what you shared such as surprise, disagreement, anger, hurt, or embarrassment, remember that this is perfectly normal and does not mean you have done something wrong or that something is happening that is not supposed to. Human beings experience a wide array of emotions and being able to express them with another person is healthy, as long as the expression of emotion is not abusive. It is not your responsibility to ensure everyone around you is comfortable all the time. Your responsibility is to stay open as you are speaking and listening in the spirit of trust, growth, and development.
- **Celebrate attempts, not perfection.** Each time you choose honesty over comfort, even if the conversation doesn't go as you wished it had, you strengthen your capacity for real connection and courageous leadership. As Nelson Mandela suggested: there is no losing. We either win or we learn. Both are valuable.

Communication Commitment #5: Practice Candor

Think about a conversation you would like to be able to have that will require you to reveal. Write your message here as succinctly as possible using unarguable language.

The reason this feels risky/What I am concerned about is . . .

If I choose to have the conversation, I will help myself reduce anxiety/fear by . . .

Demonstrate, Reward, Discourage

Let's close this chapter by circling back to the concepts you learned in Chapter 6. As a cultural architect, your three most powerful levers for influencing culture are: demonstrate, reward, discourage. This is true no matter what topic, skillset, or issue we're thinking about. So let's apply this to communication norms on your team with a short but powerful written activity that will help you acknowledge where you're already strong and where you have development opportunities.

Thinking specifically about the *communication* skills you've learned and the norms that exist on your team, reflect in writing on the following:

Demonstrate	Reward	Discourage
What am I currently demonstrating that supports my desired team culture?	What am I currently rewarding in others that supports desired culture?	What do I discourage in others to support desired culture?
What do I *need to be* demonstrating better to support desired culture?	What do I *need to be* rewarding more often to support desired culture?	What do I *need to be* discouraging more often to support desired culture?

Free resources available at: www.vidlwork.com/culturejourney book

- Managing reactivity tool: Emotional Energy Quadrants
- Managing reactivity tool: The Line
- List of our favorite books and podcasts that support effective communication
- List of Powerful Questions
- "Rumble Language" from Brene Brown

9 Navigating Conflict

Rebecca

I (Rebecca) was raised by two of the kindest people I've ever met. I often say that I won the parent lottery simply by being born to Rodney and Susan Johnson. Even as very young adults likely unprepared for the challenges of parenthood, they taught me a lot about how to live a good life, mostly by what they modeled for me. I learned lessons about kindness, empathy, patience, money, humor, storytelling, family traditions, service, and adventure that have helped me create a fulfilling adult life. (Thank you, Mom and Dad!)

Like all parents, though, even the most well-intended ones, there were a few lessons my parents could not teach me, because they simply did not yet have the knowledge or skill themselves. One of the things I did *not* learn in my early life from my parents (or my friends' parents or my neighbors or my teachers) is how to think about and navigate conflict effectively.

I didn't learn that interpersonal friction and conflict is normal, to be expected, and not inherently bad. I didn't learn that the presence of friction or conflict in a conversation or relationship does not necessarily mean something is wrong, or that the relationship will be negatively impacted by the conflict. I didn't learn that when it is handled with helpful intentions and skill, conflict can actually strengthen relationships and lead to *deeper connection*. Since there was very little overt conflict in my house and the friction that did exist was mostly under the surface and not directly addressed, I also didn't learn many of the skills necessary for navigating friction, and I didn't get many opportunities to practice how to get through the discomfort and experience the benefits on the other side. Because of this, one of my most significant adaptive challenges as a person, a parent, and a leader, has been to improve the way I navigate interpersonal friction and situational conflict. It was not until my late 30s that my life demanded that I get better at this and that I was ready to do so.

Recall from Chapter 3 that an adaptive challenge is not one that can be effectively addressed with the same inner operating system that created the challenge. For me, this adaptive challenge has required deep and broad Me Work to update my own iOS. I have had to:

- Examine old stories and previously unchecked assumptions about myself, others, relationships, and conflict
- Challenge and rewrite narratives that were no longer serving me well
- Explore my need to be liked and approved of by everyone and develop a new value proposition for myself that does not involve maintaining harmony at all costs
- Practice new skills, often poorly at first, such as speaking candidly and taking things less personally
- Practice existing with my own discomfort and other people's discomfort without shutting down or placating

At the age of 51, after years of Me Work, it feels good to be able to truthfully say that I am significantly better at speaking candidly and navigating friction and conflict. My life, my family, and my business are better because of it.

A Nearly Universal Challenge

Why am I telling you my story? Not because it's particularly unique; in fact, it's the opposite. We all have a story about conflict that influences how we think about it and navigate it everywhere, including in the workplace. My story is just one specific illustration of how experiences, inner narratives, and patterns we bring into adulthood interfere with our ability to think about and navigate conflict productively. This seems to be true for most adults. While I (Rebecca) entered adulthood with a tendency for conflict avoidance and niceness-at-all-costs, other people enter adulthood with different modus operandi. For example, some people's life experiences have taught them that engaging in even unnecessary and unhealthy conflict is "just how we show love." Others see conflict as an opportunity to prove rightness or superiority, or a fight to be "won."

In the midst of all these diverse stories and perspectives, there are nearly universal challenges we see around conflict in the workplace. Most of us misunderstand the value of conflict. We take things too personally. When situations start to feel heated or tense, we often end up doing one of several unproductive things:

- Impulsively react to our emotions in a way that shuts other people down or unnecessarily escalates the situation
- Placate, pretend, or back pedal to keep things harmonious
- Shut down or withdraw to end the vulnerability as quickly as possible

Since many adults lack the skills and practice necessary to navigate conflict well, the net result is poor for both organizational culture and performance. The teams with the strongest cultures aren't happy or harmonious all the time; they are usually the teams who collectively navigate the friction that inherently exists with grace, clarity, and skill. Teams and organizations have little chance of improving culture meaningfully if they do not get better at navigating conflict.

That's what this chapter is about.

Things You Need to Know

Whether you are a formal leader with title and high positional power committed to leading the CultureJourney, an influential leader in your organization without an "official" title, or an employee in any role wanting to know how to navigate friction better for yourself or your team, there are a few essential ideas to internalize.

First, navigating friction well requires you to put into practice the skill-sets you learned in Chapter 8. These include:

- regulate your energy to minimize reactivity and defensiveness
- lean into empathy
- listen with helpful intentions
- ask questions from a place of curiosity (instead of judgment)
- speak candidly with care using unarguable language

If you do nothing else, practicing these five key skills will go a long way in helping you and your team better navigate friction.

Second—and this is a biggie—not all conflict is the same. It's helpful to be able to differentiate and get more attuned to what type of conflict is happening. Different types of conflict require different responses.

Third, as it relates to organizational culture and performance, the necessary Me Work and We Work around culture is not only about "getting through" tense situations better but going one or two steps further: *inviting* healthy dissent when it will be helpful to the situation and *helping tense conversations* stay productive when we have influence.

Not All Conflict Is the Same

While it may be a bit of a simplification, we categorize conflict into two types.

The first type of conflict arises when people have different ideas or opinions, and those dissenting perspectives are bumping into each other. Anna thinks the right solution to the issue is A. Peter thinks the right solution is B. They both state their opinions out loud in a meeting. We call this **Idea Friction**. When differing perspectives, interpretations, assumptions, or creative insights rub together, the friction is about *what* we think. This type of friction—if navigated with curiosity, skill, and openness—creates energy and direction for innovation and better collective decisions. The trick is that, in most organizations, Idea Friction is not navigated well enough to leverage its full potential.

The second type of conflict arises when a difference in *what* we think triggers us emotionally because it touches *who we are* or *how we're seen*. We call this **Identity Friction**. It's very natural for Idea Friction to lead nearly immediately to Identity Friction, which is when the unspoken focus moves from the *issue* to *self or status*. When this happens, people shift to self-protection, proving, or withdrawal. For example, if Peter takes the conversation as a personal affront and Anna is strongly attached to being right, and neither of them has the awareness of skill to check themselves and reset, then their difference of opinion will quickly generate into Identity Friction, which will derail the conversation.

Think about a situation you have experienced recently with one or more people at work. Separate the parts of the conflict into these categories:

Idea Friction: *What* difference of thinking, ideas, or perspectives does this conflict involve? Write in unarguable language and with no drama or hyperbole.	**Identity Friction:** *How* does this difference in thinking trigger you emotionally? Use the sentence starters below. As you respond, use unarguable language with no drama or hyperbole.
Example: "Andy told me he does not think my team member is doing a good job. I think she *is* doing a good job but that he has unreasonable expectations."	Example: "When Andy said that, I felt surprised and upset. The story I am telling myself is that he is wrong. I feel a strong need to show him he's wrong and to protect my team members from other people's disapproval."
The other person's idea or perspective seems to be that . . .	*This difference of opinion makes me feel . . .*
	What feels like it might be at risk is . . .
My idea or perspective is that	
	What I might be defending or protecting against is . . .

Inviting Dissent and Keeping It Productive

Cultural architects understand that the way a team or organization handles dissent tells the truth about its culture far more than its slogans or stated values do. A team that can disagree openly and productively is a team that trusts itself. Especially as a cultural architect, your role is not only to navigate conflict when it happens but also to intentionally foster a team culture where healthy dissent is welcomed and skillfully managed. As always, this requires you to use your three levers: demonstrate, reward, and discourage. You must *demonstrate* the willingness to hear what's hard to hear and the ability to keep conversations moving toward learning instead of blame or defensiveness. You'll need to *reward* helpful conflict resolution behaviors when you see them and *discourage* the opposite.

Inviting dissent is an ongoing practice but may be especially important early on in teams where fear, politeness, or over-valuing harmony has kept dissent to a minimum. You might invite dissent by:

- **Routinely asking for counterpoints.** "What might we be missing?" or "Who sees this differently?" After asking questions like this, stay open and receptive, even if you are triggered by or disagree with what comes up in response.
- **Reward healthy dissent.** When a team member offers a dissenting opinion, especially if it's someone who typically does not, recognize it. Something as simple as "Thank you for sharing that perspective, Felix. I know it can feel hard to express disagreement."

While inviting dissent is important, without clear norms for how to *stay* in Idea Friction while minimizing Identity Friction, the invited dissent can quickly devolve or make the team feel less psychologically safe. When dissent emerges, leaders who act as cultural architects help to keep it productive. For example, they might:

- **Frame the purpose.** Before the discussion gets too heated, remind people *why* dissent is important and what the purpose of the conversation is. "The fact that we have different opinions is valuable because it can help us get to the decision that is in the best interest of the organization. As we navigate this, let's remember that we're not debating to win; we're exploring to understand."

- **Anchor to something greater.** People can often work through Identity Friction more quickly when they are tethered to something larger than their individual egos, like the mission, the values, the customer, or the community. You might say something like, "This is an important conversation because it can potentially lead to the resolution of an issue that is affecting the citizens we serve. Let's keep that mission front and center as we think about the best resolution for our city."

Over time, these practices build a shared muscle: the ability to stay connected and constructive even when perspectives collide. This is not just a communication skill; it's a competency necessary for designing and nurturing intentional cultures. When dissent is normalized and managed well, it strengthens trust, accelerates learning, and increases the organization's capacity to adapt.

Me Work and We Work

As with all challenges, to get better at inviting and navigating conflict productively, we can think about commitments through the lens of Me Work and We Work.

Me Work

Navigating conflict is an area that often requires significant Me Work. It might require that we confront our own discomfort with being questioned, our attachment to being right, and our reflex to control outcomes. It takes humility and courage to say, "Tell me what you see that I don't," and then stay open to the answer. Here are a few suggestions that can help guide your Me Work:

1. **Use this language with yourself:** Learn to pause and ask, "Am I in *Idea Friction* or has this turned into *Identity Friction*?" This is a simple self-check that moves you from reaction to reflection.
2. **Regulate before responding:** Notice emotional cues of defensiveness and use breath, posture, or another technique to reduce reactivity before responding. (Review 8 if you need a refresher on reducing

defensiveness.) If you need more than a momentary pause to respond well, say so and take the time you need.

3. **Assume best intent:** Remind yourself that most people are operating with positive intentions most of the time. Pay attention to your tendency to take things personally too often.
4. **Use unarguable language:** Practice describing your experience with language that represents what is true for you right now. ("It sounds like we have a difference of opinion. I can feel myself getting defensive but I'm committed to staying in curiosity. The story I'm telling myself is . . .") Revisit 8 if you need a refresher on this.

We Work

Very few teams have mastered the art and skill of navigating dissent productively. This is likely to be a needed area of focus for your team as well. Ideas for possible We Work include:

1. **Develop common language and understanding:** Share these terms with your team and what you are learning about the difference between Idea and Identify friction. Discuss how you might collectively use these concepts to invite and navigate conflict better together.
2. **Establish explicit guidelines:** Discuss and align on commitments for how you agree to behave together specifically in this area. Post those commitments in places where dissenting conversations are likely to happen. Revisit them often.
3. **Embed these concepts in everyday process:** For example, you might include Idea versus Identity Friction questions in debrief templates, supervision conversations, or team learning sessions.
4. **Offer training and coaching for skill development:** Recognizing that most people are lacking skills and practice in this area, participate in a formal facilitated training where you can learn and skill up together. Offer professional coaching services for those who need more.

While most individuals and teams need work in this area, the work is well worth it. We've seen leaders and teams learn to navigate dissent well. Let's see what happens when they do.

Taryn

Taryn is a high-level leader in county government. She leads the team that handles permits. Her team is short-staffed right now and they are facing a six-week backlog in permit approvals. Complaints have been stacking up and Taryn's boss has been asking pointed questions. The team is feeling overworked and especially pressured about this issue. So Taryn schedules an issue-resolution session with her direct reports. Because the team has just learned about Idea versus Identity Friction and are newly practicing together, Taryn asks us to join to the meeting to help them navigate what she knows will be a friction-filled meeting. It turns out she needs little support from us.

After a few minutes dedicated to checking in and personal connection with each other, Taryn reminds her team about the purpose of the meeting and the skills they learned together in a previous Vidl Work training about navigating conflict.

"I know this has been a tough time and stress is high. We have several pressing issues to resolve and different ideas about how to do that. That's good. Today is about surfacing the best thinking, not winning. I think our conversation will be more productive if we all keep in mind what we learned about Idea Friction versus Identity Friction. As we debate how best to move forward given the circumstances, pay attention to your intentions and your reactions. Let's start with the permit issue. I'd like to hear everyone's thinking."

Maya starts. "I don't see a way for us to reduce backlog unless we freeze new non-essential applications for two weeks and reassign reviewers to the oldest files. We have to stop the influx or we'll just keep drowning."

Luis leans forward. "I'm concerned that freezing applications will make the community even angrier than they are now and they'll kill us on social media. We'll create a bigger political problem. I think we should go first-in/first-out for fairness and consider adding weekend hours for the next month."

Frowning, Devon says, "There's no way we can do that. Our office staff can't handle weekend hours on top of everything else we've been through. We're already stretched and morale is low. Besides, the bottleneck is in the field, not intake."

Priya exhales and says, "It's not just the field employees; our office staff are a huge part of the problem too. We have a few people who aren't carrying their weight and that's slowing things down further. That team needs stronger leadership and someone who will hold them accountable."

Taryn seems to notice the shift in energy in the room because she holds up her hand and calmly says "Pause."

"I notice I'm getting tense. The story I'm telling myself is that we're starting to move from what we think to who's to blame. That tells me we're sliding into Identity Friction."

Silence. Then a few nods.

Taryn goes to the white board and draws two columns: "Idea Friction" and "Identity Friction." "Let's get our ideas on the board along with what's unspoken about them. I'm going to ask each of you two questions. First, state your idea in one sentence. Second, name what feels at risk for you personally in this conversation. I'm not asking you to defend anything. Just name it."

As each leader shares their response and is able to identify and name what they are defending, the energy in the room shifts again. The conversation continues with what feels like more humility and courage, away from blame and anchored in a higher purpose.

Within an hour, the team not only generates a blended plan for reducing the backlog; they have done so with trust and connection preserved. By naming what felt personally at risk, the team lowered the emotional temperature enough to think more clearly. What started as a near-spiral into identity friction ended as a shared commitment: protect the relationships, challenge ideas, and move forward together. The skill didn't eliminate the workload, but it unlocked better thinking under pressure.

In Summary

Navigating conflict well is one of the essential cultural muscles that separates strong teams from struggling ones. When people can surface differences, stay in Idea Friction, regulate Identity Friction, and move through discomfort with candor, curiosity, and connection, they create the conditions in which trust, learning, and healthy dissent can thrive. But even the most skillful conflict navigation will fall short if the behaviors that undermine culture—defensiveness, avoidance, blame, disrespect, or repeated violations of agreed-upon norms—are tolerated. The next chapter turns to the discipline that holds all of this together: accountability.

10 Accountability

In previous chapters, we've explored concepts for designing and nurturing an intentional culture, including psychological safety, effective communication, and navigating conflict productively. But none of these concepts mean much if the behaviors associated with them aren't demonstrated regularly—or if the opposite, undermining behaviors are repeatedly tolerated. This is where accountability comes in.

In the early stages of intentional culture work, people often assume this is "soft skills" work focused primarily on helping people treat each other with more kindness and respect. While it's true that meaningful culture change results in warmer, kinder environments and relationships, culture work can also be uncomfortable and hard. This becomes especially true when we start talking about accountability.

If you're a formal leader, you carry extra responsibility around accountability. Not only is it essential that you demonstrate full ownership of your role, your inner operating system, and your actions—it's also imperative that you address situations where accountability is missing. Let's pause on this point.

When talking about accountability, we used to use language like "holding others accountable," but we now think about accountability differently. As our team member Michelle Spher[1] once said casually in conversation, "You can't really hold another person accountable." This was a light bulb moment for me (Rebecca) because I hadn't thought about it that way before, but I immediately saw the truth in it. As we explored in Chapter 5, the only thing we ever truly can control is ourselves. This means that each of us can choose to take responsibility for our thoughts, feelings, decisions, actions, and reactions—but we can't *make* other people take responsibility for theirs. However, we can create conditions in which accountability is expected, supported, and rewarded and where the opposite is discouraged, at least within our spheres of influence.

In this chapter, we'll introduce a framework for thinking about accountability called the Four Cs: clear expectations, clear capability, clear feedback, and clear consequences. Like all frameworks, this one is only valuable if you put it to use. Knowing it intellectually won't make you an accountable person or solve accountability issues for you, but it will give you a structured and effective model for thinking about your options, responsibilities, commitments, and practices—and for increasing the chances that accountability improves on your team.

Right People. Right Seats

Before we get into the framework, there's an important concept at the heart of accountability. In his book, *Good to Great,* Jim Collins originally referred to this idea as "getting the right people on the bus and getting those people in the right seats."[2] Later, in his book *Traction,* CEO and author Gino Wickman furthered the conversation and used the phrase "right people, right seats."[3] For our purposes, we'll use "right people, right seats."

> **In our experience, once you have the right people in the right seats, much of your culture work is already done—and what remains becomes far easier.**

Read that last sentence again and sit with it for a moment. It's one of the most important sentences in this book.

What does the phrase "right people, right seats" means? Let's break it down.

Right people. Knowing whether someone is the right person requires clarity about your core values. When values are clear, you can more easily see who naturally aligns with them and who consistently struggles to act in ways that undermine or threaten your desired culture. It becomes much easier to hire, coach, and, when necessary, part ways with people based on shared expectations rather than subjective impressions. (We devote the next chapter to defining desired culture through core values.)

Right seats. When someone is in the right seat, it means their current strengths, skills, and capabilities align well with the functional responsibilities of the role they are in. They understand the nuances of the job and know how to do what it requires. They *want* to be in this role right now. And they have the time, energy, and physical capacity to do it well. When someone is not in the right seat, they feel it, everyone around them feels it, and both culture and business performance suffer.[4]

The concept of right people, right seats leads naturally to the idea that we each hold responsibility for two types of accountability: performance and cultural.

Performance accountability is the "what" of our work. Are we tending to the tasks, projects, processes, responsibilities, and outcomes our job requires? Are we completing responsibilities with quality and on time? Are our skills and capabilities a good match for the role we're in? This is the type of accountability that most organizations try to address through employee performance evaluations.

Cultural accountability is the "how." Not just how we do our jobs, but how we relate to each other and to external stakeholders as we do them. Are we doing our Me Work and We Work? Behaving in ways that foster psychological safety? Practicing effective communication and cleaning up misunderstandings when they occur? Learning to navigate friction better? Embodying our organization's core values in our daily behaviors?

Both forms of accountability matter, and both must be present for someone to truly be the "right person in the right seat." In nearly every client we have ever worked with, we have seen misalignments in both directions—and associated challenges with each scenario.

Scenario 1: Right person, wrong seat. We see employees who are culturally aligned and relate well with others but are not performing their job well. In these scenarios, the challenge leaders face is that it often feels unkind to address performance issues head on when the employee is "nice" or seemingly trying hard. But even the nicest of people trying their best, if left in the wrong seat, will inadvertently cause friction, undermine culture, and limit the team's potential.

Scenario 2: Right seat, questionable/wrong person. Conversely, we see employees who do their job extremely well, often called "high performers," who are undermining culture with poor behavior. This scenario often feels daunting to leaders too; they avoid addressing the employee's behavior for fear of backlash or losing them to another organization. But here's an important truth about this: ***If a person in your organization repeatedly behaves in ways that undermine culture and is not able or willing to evolve, no degree of high performance is worth keeping them because of the cultural damage they do in the long term.***[5]

Mark's story underscores this point.

Mark

Mark was a senior manager for a global firm I (Natalie) worked with. Mark's influence far exceeded his title. He was a high performer by every traditional measure. He brought in significant clients, worked long hours, and consistently delivered results.

Culturally though, he was costly. Over time, I learned that Mark was brash and dismissive. He interrupted people, corrected them publicly, and used sarcasm when things didn't go his way. Under pressure, his tone turned aggressive. People around Mark learned quickly that staying quiet was safer than speaking up. Turnover on his team was high, and colleagues avoided working with him whenever possible. I worked with this team for several years and was always amazed at how long this went on.

For years, Mark was only held accountable for his performance, not for his impact on culture. He delivered results so it was a long time before Human Resources was even brought in to help. But even when an occasional HR conversation happened, there was only brief improvement, followed by the same patterns. Meanwhile, the organization absorbed the cost of delaying cultural accountability:

- Years of disengagement and unnecessary turnover on Mark's team
- Significant leadership and HR energy spent managing around one person
- Fear, silence, and emotional exhaustion on teams
- Missed opportunities for collaboration, learning, and growth

The Four Cs

The Four Cs framework can be used to think about both types of accountability. Since this is a book about culture, we'll focus primarily on how this framework applies to cultural accountability, though you'll quickly see the parallels to performance as well. Here are the Four Cs (see Figure 10.1):

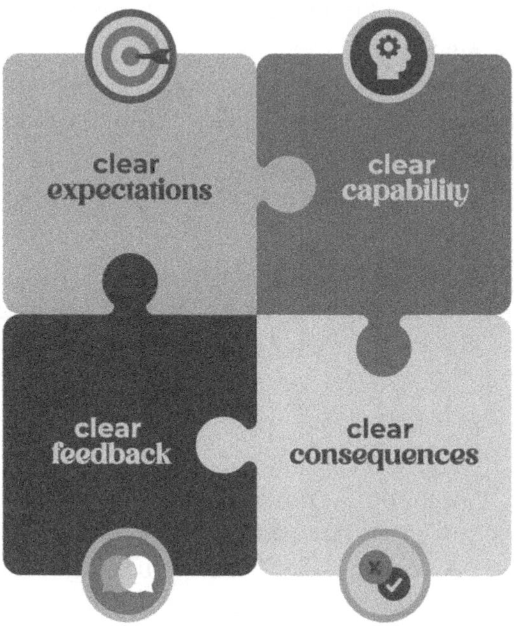

FIGURE 10.1 The four Cs of accountability.

Notice that the Four Cs all start with the same word: **clear**. That's purposeful because clarity is essential for designing and nurturing an intentional culture. Unfortunately, we humans are not great at creating clarity for ourselves and with other people, so many of us have Me Work and We Work to do. While we know that "clear is kind," we see and hear about the effects of lack of clarity frequently. Wade's story is a recent example.

Wade

Wade is a senior leader in a pharmaceutical company. While his team is full of talented people, he has felt increasingly frustrated with one team member, Connor, who seems to be undermining psychological safety on the team and shutting down others.

In a coaching session, Wade shares his frustration: "Connor interrupts people all the time. I've even seen him literally roll his eyes a few times. The team shuts down around him. I notice people coming to me after meetings are over to share ideas and I think it's because they're afraid of the reaction they'll get from Connor."

Over the next few minutes, I (Natalie) ask Wade about the Four Cs. *Has he made his behavioral expectations explicitly clear? Does he think Connor has the capability to meet those expectations? Has he given Connor direct and timely feedback? What consequences is Connor experiencing as a result of his behavior?*

Initially, Wade responds the way many leaders do, with a sense of exasperation: "I haven't explicitly called him out on these behaviors, but I've circled around it. The man is 50 years old. Shouldn't he *know* how to behave?"

The First C: Clear Expectations

Think about a source of tension you are experiencing in your life right now involving someone who is not behaving the way you want them to be. Maybe your child is spending too much time attached to technology.

Or your neighbor repeatedly parks his car too close to your driveway so you can't get out. Or your team member talks loudly near you making it hard to focus. Or someone who reports to you often generates unnecessary drama in meetings. As you think about this source of tension, ask yourself: *How sure am I that this person is explicitly clear about my expectations?*

Many problems, tensions, and misunderstandings are the result of lack of clear expectations. Since most of us aren't very good at consistently clarifying our expectations, we are often frustrated when others aren't behaving according to those expectations. I (Rebecca) heard someone describe this in easy terms recently when talking about a conversation she had with her husband who said to her: "Honey, I think you have stories in your head right now about how this should go and I either need to know those stories or you need to stop being upset with me for *not* knowing those stories."

We often ask people in group trainings *why* we humans fail to be clear about our expectations with others. The answers come easily:

- *We assumed they knew so we didn't explicitly say it.*
- *We said it out loud but didn't confirm the other person received the message as we intended it.*
- *We don't actually have mental clarity for ourselves so couldn't create it for others.*
- *We don't make time to do so.*
- *We are concerned other people will perceive us as too cold, harsh, or rigid if we state our expectations directly and in plain language.*

Think about yourself. If you are aware that you fail to make your expectations clear to others, at least on occasion, pause for a moment and consider why. If you really pause and think, you'll likely realize you have some Me Work to do in this area.

When it comes to people's behavior and interpersonal dynamics, creating clarity around expectations is essential. Whether you are a formal leader or an employee at any level, there is opportunity for you here and you have options:

Practice	Formal Leaders	Employees at All Levels
Establish shared agreements about how we behave together.	One of the strongest ways leaders can create clarity is by guiding the group in forming explicit behavioral guidelines or relying on existing guidelines. The next chapter is dedicated to this topic. If specific guidelines have not yet been formalized, leaders can prompt the group in specific situations. For example, you might ask, "We're under a lot of stress right now. Let's talk about what behaviors we want to see from each other, and what behaviors we'll do our best to minimize." Once you have verbal agreement, ensure these behaviors are captured in writing and easily seen by all team members.	Even without a formal title, any team member can say, "I'd love to make sure we have shared expectations about how we want to navigate this together. Would it be helpful to talk about what good teamwork looks like for us?"

Practice	Formal Leaders	Employees at All Levels
Clarify roles, decision rights, and boundaries to reduce unnecessary interpersonal friction.	It is the responsibility of the leader of a group to initiate conversations related to who owns what. When discussing a project, you might say, "Let's be explicit about who is responsible, who needs to be consulted, and what decisions require group alignment." By clarifying these ambiguous decision points up front, we eliminate the guesswork, accidental overstepping, or ball-dropping that often undermines culture.	When you don't have clarity, ask for it. For example, you might ask, "Can you clarify for me what decisions you're expecting I will make on my own, and what decisions I need input on?" These questions create shared understanding and normalize the act of seeking clarity rather than pretending to have it. By modeling this type of clarity-seeking behavior, you encourage others to do the same.
Check for clarity	After giving direction, providing information, or discussing expectations, pause to check for shared meaning. Not a quiz, but an alignment moment: "I want to ensure we both have clarity here. What are you taking away from this?"	Whether you are giving direction or receiving it, aim for clarity. If you're receiving direction, you might say, "I'd like to say back what I think we agreed on to make sure I heard it correctly." And then repeat it back in your own words.
Invite and normalize questions	Especially with complex information or issues that might create unexpressed resistance, invite questions in a way that conveys that you expect questions and welcome them. You might ask: "We've talked about a lot today. Let's spend the rest of our time together addressing your questions. What else do you need or want to know?"	At any level of employment, you can invite and normalize questions. If you're working on a project with a colleague and suspect you might have a clarity issue, you can simply ask, "Can we check in today and make sure we're on the same page with who's doing what on this project?"

(Continued)

Practice	Formal Leaders	Employees at All Levels
Reinforce clarity when needed	Name gaps before they snowball and create more frustration as time goes on: "We agreed to start meetings on time, and I'm noticing we haven't been holding that line. What needs to change?"	Team members can reduce tension by naming their preferences or expectations instead of hoping others infer them: "Since we agreed to truly disconnect on evenings and weekends, I'm trying not to check email at all during those times. If there's something you really need me to know during our downtime, give me a call because I won't see an email."
Ritualize clarity moments	Consider building small routines that demonstrate your commitment to clarity and reward others for doing their part. For example, you might consistently open meetings with team agreements, check in monthly on how the team is doing against their commitments, or end projects with reflections on where more clarity would have been helpful and how to do better next time.	What rituals and routines might help you give or get clarity around expectations when you need it? Perhaps you commit to ending each meeting with your leader or colleagues by stating a brief recap to ensure you're aligned or asking a question like "Is there anything else I should know?"

The Second C: Clear Capability

The second C is clear **capability**. This is an idea that's often overlooked even though it's frequently at the heart of our frustrations around lack of accountability.

Clear capability means that, anytime we are expecting a person or group to do something or behave a certain way, we need to be sure their current capability will allow them to deliver on those expectations. If we don't know, we find out. If the answer is "no," then what's the plan? There is nothing more frustrating than being expected to deliver on something you simply cannot—or repeatedly waiting for someone to meet expectations they won't be able to.

With performance accountability, this means we need to make sure that the person or group has the knowledge, skills, and resources to meet the expectations. For example, if your expectation is that your new analyst delivers a weekly metrics report with clear insights and visualizations, you need to confirm they actually know how to pull the data from the new system, interpret it accurately, and use the reporting tools your team prefers. If it turns out they've never been trained on the reporting tool or aren't confident in data interpretation, then the issue isn't a lack of accountability—it's a gap in capability. The plan might involve pairing them with a more experienced teammate for a few cycles, giving them training on the system, or reallocating certain tasks until they're fully up to speed.

With cultural capability, we're no longer talking about technical skills and knowledge or external resources; we're talking about our own inner operating systems. When someone on our team is undermining culture with their behavior and we have made our expectations explicitly clear but they are still operating the same way, we have to ask ourselves: *Is this person capable of demonstrating the behaviors necessary for supporting our desired culture? Is the problem that they just have not experienced the right feedback or consequences—or do we have a capability issue?*

We don't ask this question from a standpoint of judgment, superiority, or disdain, but with the recognition that people are at different points on their self-development journeys. We honor the fact that our organization is requesting a certain standard of behavior that not everyone will be able to consistently model right away—and that's normal and to be expected.

For example, let's say your organization is focused on fostering a set of desirable behaviors that include "Speak candidly, with care." Some people will already be comfortable with and in the habit of speaking candidly with care. Some will need shared language, skills, practice, and reinforcement through group norms. Others will find this behavior incredibly difficult to demonstrate due to deeply ingrained resistance, much of which was formed long before they came to work on your team—predispositions they were born with, prior life experiences, habitual thinking patterns, unaddressed adaptive challenges, development opportunities they have or have not had, etc. It just depends on their current iOS, how big their development gap is, and how intensively they are able and willing to do their Me Work.

What Do You Do When You Have a Capability Gap?

When someone lacks the current capability to consistently demonstrate the cultural behaviors your organization expects, the goal isn't to judge or rescue them—it's to support their development while also protecting the culture. A behavioral capability gap isn't a character flaw; it's simply an indication of where someone is in their Me Work.

If you are a formal leader and you have identified a capability gap that is currently making it difficult for a team member to align well with values, you must attend to this. For the good of the organization, the person needs to either develop reasonably soon or be removed from this seat or the organization. Here's where the next two Cs in the framework become especially important.

The Third C: Clear Feedback

Let's go back to Wade.

As the coaching conversation with Wade progresses, it becomes clear that he has not made behavioral expectations clear to Connor. His first step is to have a clarifying conversation with Connor to let him know how his interrupting and eye-rolling are negatively impacting the team and outlining what he expects instead. As part of this conversation, he'll need to assess in partnership with Connor whether Connor feels he can make these changes quickly. In this instance, the answer is likely yes. This in itself is a feedback conversation. Preferably, the conversation feels like a two-way street with a "loop" of feedback happening in both directions.

As time goes on, Wade will need to offer Connor feedback at least one more time. If Connor's behavior improves, Wade will ideally offer Connor validating feedback in private. He might say something reinforcing and rewarding like "I notice a big difference in meetings lately. Thank you for adjusting." If Connor continues to align with values in this way, nothing more needs to be said. However, if Connor's undermining behavior continues, Wade will need to offer a different type of feedback.

When you need to offer feedback in response to undermining behaviors, here are some ideas to consider:

- **Consistently model the behavior yourself.** By now, you're familiar with how important it is for you to demonstrate what you want to see in others. Enough said.
- **Tap into your communication basics (from** Chapter 8). Remember these five essentials: regulate your energy to minimize ego and defensiveness, connect with empathy, listen with intention, ask powerful questions, and speak candidly using unarguable language.
- **Name the specific behavior gap with compassion and clarity.** Avoid vague feedback ("You need to be more collaborative") and anchor the conversation in observable behaviors ("When people share new ideas with you, I observe you quickly dismissing them or focusing on why they won't work.")
- **Provide tools, language, or frameworks that make the behavior learnable.** Some people simply haven't been exposed to the practices you're asking for, in which case they need shared language and skill-building. This is one of the reasons providing group training and professional coaching is an essential component of culture transformation. Identify together what investment is needed to help this person bridge the capability gap.
- **Identify practice opportunities.** Behavior change requires reps. Invite them to practice this new behavior in scenarios that are less tense or likely to create stress.
- **Be explicit about what improvement looks like.** Define the small indicators of progress so the person can recognize and build on them.

- **Hold the line with compassion.** If the person is unwilling or unable to do the work required, you can still treat them with dignity while making decisions that protect team safety and culture. This is true even when protecting the culture requires removing them from the organization. This isn't punitive; it's stewardship.

The Fourth C: Clear Consequences

For many of us, the word "consequences" conjures up a sense of negativity and makes us immediately think about things we don't want, like punishment or discipline. But consequences are not inherently negative and can be positive. A consequence is just what happens *after* something else, whether it's a logical conclusion, an outcome, or a simple effect. Consequences can also be naturally occurring or purposefully applied. Here's a list of common consequences that might naturally occur or be purposefully applied in the workplace based on a person's repeated behavior.

Positive Consequences for Supportive Behavior and/or High Performance	**Negative Consequences for Unsupportive Behavior and/or Lower Performance**
Naturally occurring: • Sense of pride/accomplishment in self • More positive results/outcomes • Recognition and gratitude from others • Opportunities/involvement in new projects • Positive impact on well-being	*Naturally occurring:* • Poor feelings about self (frustration, embarrassment, guilt) • Less positive results/outcomes • Disapproval or negative judgment from others • Disconnection from team(s)
Purposefully applied: • Verbal recognition in private and public • Promotion • Awards • Pay raises or bonuses	*Purposefully applied:* • Being removed from meaningful projects • Performance Improvement Plan • Demotion • Missing opportunity for compensation increase • Removal from organization

If you're a formal leader, you have extra responsibility around ensuring that your team members are experiencing consequences that reward and discourage appropriately. Of course, you only have control over yourself—what and how you think, say, and do—but there is a lot of opportunity in just this realm.

Positive consequences. When team members are demonstrating supportive behaviors and meeting or exceeding expectations, you can influence the degree to which they feel rewarded and experience positive consequences. For example, imagine a team member who consistently invites quieter voices into meetings, asks thoughtful questions, and follows through on commitments. In addition to the natural satisfaction they may feel from doing good work, you can purposefully amplify the positive consequences by naming these behaviors in real time, recognizing them publicly in a team meeting, or inviting that person to take on a visible role in an upcoming project. This is the type of person who also should be prioritized for rewarding with financial compensation whenever possible too. Over time, these signals reinforce not just *what* results are valued, but *how* those results are achieved.

Negative consequences. When team members are undermining culture or chronically missing performance expectations, you can influence the degree to which they are experiencing negative consequences. There's an important caveat about this last statement, though. *As a formal leader, you should only move to negative consequences once you can say for sure you have done your part with the first three Cs.* It's not fair to move to disciplinary action if you aren't 100% sure you've clarified expectations, addressed capability gaps, and given adequate, candid feedback. Conversely, if you feel confident the first three Cs have been attended to well and you are still having cultural alignment or performance issues, then you *must* move to negative consequences. For example, consider a team member who repeatedly interrupts others, dismisses feedback, or creates defensiveness in meetings despite multiple clear conversations about expectations and impact. If the behavior continues, allowing them to remain in high-visibility roles or on critical projects sends a message that the behavior is acceptable. A more aligned response might be removing them from those opportunities, formally documenting the issue, or initiating a performance improvement plan—making it clear that continued misalignment will affect their role or future with the organization.

In Summary

In this chapter, we've explored why accountability is essential to designing and nurturing an intentional culture—and why it's not something you can force on others, but something you create the conditions for, starting with yourself. We underscored the importance of "right people, right seats," highlighting the importance of both cultural alignment and role fit, and why strong performance never justifies behavior that undermines culture. We introduced you to the Four Cs framework—clear expectations, clear capability, clear feedback, and clear consequences—as a practical way to think about your responsibility for accountability, whether you're a formal leader or not.

We'll close this chapter by acknowledging that accountability is one of the hardest parts of culture work—and of life in general. Being an accountable person requires commitment, discipline, and practice. The same is true for creating the conditions where accountability in other people emerges and is rewarded and where the opposite is discouraged. For many of us, increasing accountability in ourselves and others is a lifelong practice requiring a great deal of Me Work and We Work. While it presents a significant and sometimes uncomfortable growth opportunity, it's also the path to less frustration, more connection, and greater performance.

11 Defining Desired Culture

Victoria

I (Natalie) am meeting with Victoria, the VP of HR at an organization exploring what we have to offer. She describes the challenges the team is facing and what feels like their biggest barrier.

"It feels like we're trying to improve culture in a vague, unmeasurable way," she says. "We use words like 'positive culture' and 'healthy workplace', but what do those actually mean? We'd never create a strategic plan without clear metrics. How can we expect success in culture work when we don't even know what success looks like?"

Victoria is right.

From General to Specific

Everything you've learned in this book so far applies broadly to workplace culture. The good news is that culture can be improved anywhere when we apply the Me-We-Systems framework and the related concepts we've covered, including psychological safety, communication, conflict resolution, and accountability. No matter your organization, these tools can help improve relationships, the daily work experience, team dynamics, and overall performance.

But culture work becomes faster, clearer, and more impactful when you tailor it to your organization's unique context. That means defining your desired future culture and establishing ways to assess both your current reality and progress over time.

When organizations begin or reinvest in culture work, employees at all levels of the organization naturally ask questions like:

- What are we aiming for exactly?
- What kind of culture are we trying to create?
- How will we know if we've succeeded?

These questions reflect healthy curiosity and the human desire to understand where we're going before we fully get on board. To lead effectively and engage others in the process, you must be able to answer these questions.

That's what this chapter is about.

Start with the End in Mind

Most organizations have strategic plans with clear goals and measurable outcomes. They define what success looks like and then work toward it. The same principle applies to culture.

But how do we define "desired culture" in a way that's measurable and meaningful? There's no single right way, but through years of experience, we've landed on a simple, powerful formula. It includes three interconnected elements:

- Clearly defined values
- Observable behaviors
- Individual experiences

Here's the chain reaction that brings culture to life:

1. **Values** define what we believe is most deeply important—what we'll prioritize and sacrifice, even when it's hard.

2. **Behaviors** are how we demonstrate (or not) our commitment to these values on a daily basis.
3. **Experiences** are how people feel as a result of the behaviors we collectively demonstrate, reward, and discourage on a regular basis.

When we focus on clarifying and aligning these three elements, culture work becomes more tangible, more directed, and more measurable. Let's start with values.

The Value of Values

If talking about organizational values makes you roll your eyes, hang in there. You're not alone. Values often feel overused, empty, or ineffective, mostly because they haven't been utilized well in the workplace. By the end of this chapter, you'll know both *why* they are important and *how* to create values that genuinely have impact.

The truth is that values matter all the time. They matter even in on "typical" days because, if used effectively, they help us figure out how to choose and how to be—what to prioritize and what to let go of. Since most of us make literally hundreds of decisions every day, it's helpful to have something bigger than us guide those decisions.

But values matter most when work gets hard. Periods of disruption like digital transformation, system issues, or rapid growth put pressure on every part of an organization. In those moments, instability is created. Without a clear foundation, culture becomes reactive and inconsistent, shaped more by urgency and reactivity than by intention.

That foundation is values.

When values are clear and operationalized, they provide steady ground in the middle of uncertainty. They help teams decide *how* to move forward when the path isn't obvious and *what not to sacrifice* when everything feels urgent. Values don't remove complexity, but they create connection and direction, especially when people are stressed, emotionally charged, or navigating system issues.

I (Natalie) saw this play out in a healthcare system that was undergoing digital transformation. New technology was rolled out quickly to improve efficiency, but teams were overwhelmed, frustrated, and afraid of making mistakes. Instead of focusing solely on technology, leaders anchored decisions in one core value: *care for people first*. That value shaped behaviors, helped teams make decisions while inviting feedback early on. This normalized a learning curve instead of striving for perfection or penalizing when people made mistakes. The system changed, but trust remained intact, and engagement rebounded faster than expected.

The Trouble with Values

Despite their potential, values often *underwhelm*. There are reasons for that. Let's look at where organizations often go wrong—and how to do better.

Historically, values have been chosen somewhat arbitrarily, often landing on familiar words like respect, integrity, and honesty. While these are good and necessary qualities, they're also baseline expectations, not distinctive cultural commitments. Too often, leaders expect these generic words to solve complex culture challenges or change people's behavior simply by saying them out loud and hanging them on walls. Of course, that's not how it works.

Here are some common pitfalls we've seen with organizational values:

1. **Lack of clarity.** Some organizations never clearly define what's most important about how people agree to behave together. They haven't invested the time and energy into establishing clarity around what values are so important that they will ultimately determine how we choose what we prioritize and what we sacrifice.
2. **Clarity without application.** According to a 2020 study published in *MIT Sloan Management Review*, many organizations, especially large ones, *have* invested in establishing values,[1] but they have no real influence on daily behavior, decisions, or culture. Sometimes the values were established in an inner circle leadership group but not communicated well to employees. Sometimes the values were communicated early on but then mostly forgotten. Other times, the values were communicated widely and are physically visible to employees

but still go relatively unused because they are not ingrained in daily conversations. A 2018 study in the UK investigating the impact of values found that at least half of employees in organizations with existing values can't recite them.[2] In our experience, this number is higher. Whatever the exact number is, this means that most employees can't be making good use of values because they don't even know what they are!

3. **Disconnection from culture.** Even when values are well-defined, they're often not tied directly to culture initiatives. From our perspective, this is a big miss. Values are a succinct way to develop a definition of a desired culture. When we don't use them that way and instead describe culture with different language, we end up with multiple, competing lists of "important words." This brings us to number four.
4. **Too many competing words.** Some organizations overload people with long mission and vision statements, plus lists of values, principles, and priorities. One client we worked with had several different sets of "important words" designed to guide behavior: six organizational values, plus six "desired interpersonal competencies," plus various organizational goals like civility, inclusivity, and respect. Research indicates that, because of the average brain capacity of most humans, the desired number of values is three or four. More than four and we begin to confuse and dilute. Additionally, sticking to a short list of values forces us to make hard decisions about what's really important to our unique organization *right now in its journey*. When we establish too many behavioral priorities, none of them actually gets prioritized.
5. **Lack of operationalization.** Values remain abstract and unlikely to guide interpersonal dynamics unless we define specific, observable behaviors that represent these behaviors and create shared agreement on what we will demonstrate, reward, and discourage. Without this step, values can't shape how people actually work together.
6. **No measurement.** Finally, few organizations have meaningful ways to measure whether they're living their values in practice. You can find a step-by-step guide to assessing values alignment on our website.

Making Values Useful

If you decide to establish or refine existing organizational values as your method of defining desired culture, your investment of time and energy will be best used if you keep the following considerations in mind.

1. **Strategic alignment**: Values should directly support the organization's long-term goals and strategic priorities. *Ask: If we lived this value consistently, would it help us achieve our strategy faster or more effectively?*
2. **Cultural differentiation**: They should distinctly describe the culture you want, not generic traits every organization claims. *Ask: Does this uniquely describe how we want our workplace culture to feel in a way that differentiates us from our competitors?*
3. **True to identity (aspirational but authentic)**: Values should stretch the organization toward its desired culture but still be connected to its real DNA, strengths, and stories. *Ask: Can we tell stories from the past year where this value has already shown up?*
4. **Operational**: A value is only useful if it can be translated into visible, learnable, repeatable behaviors. (More on this later in the chapter.) *Ask: Can we describe at least two specific behaviors that demonstrate this value—and at least two that do not?*
5. **Practical and action-relevant**: Values should help employees navigate real-world tradeoffs and decisions, especially those with ambiguity or competing priorities. *Ask: If two priorities conflict, would this value help us choose? Does this value help us make hard decisions?*
6. **Understandable and memorable**: Values should be written in succinct, plain language and avoid corporate jargon. *Ask: Would employees remember this after hearing it just once or twice?*
7. **Emerged from broad input**: Values are more meaningful and sustainable when they reflect what people say they need to thrive. *Ask: Does this value reflect what our people say they need to thrive?*

From Words to Behaviors

Values only become powerful when they are translated into action—when people can recognize what they look like, sound like, and feel like in daily interactions, and when people hold themselves and others accountable to the higher standard required. For example, if our value is collaboration, we might deliberately identify and agree to:

- Demonstrate and reward:
  - Sharing information freely
  - Inviting input early
  - Giving credit publicly
- Minimize and discourage:
  - Hoarding information
  - Disagreeing privately after agreeing publicly
  - Competing for visibility

Operationalizing values gives everyone a shared language for what "living our values" actually means. It turns culture from something soft and vague into something concrete and measurable.

Further, when we behave in ways that align with shared values, we create the conditions for positive individual experiences with each other that are at the heart of culture.

As you are considering supportive and unsupportive behaviors you might align with each value to define desired culture, consider these criteria:

- **High impact:** Choose behaviors that, if consistently practiced or reduced would *most* move the organization toward closer alignment with that particular value. *Ask: If we only changed this behavior, would we notice a meaningful shift?*
- **Frequent and observable:** Prioritize behaviors that regularly show up in the real life of your teams instead of rare or dramatic moments. *Ask: Do people see or feel this behavior daily or at least weekly?*

- **Teachable and learnable:** A priority behavior should be something that can be taught and learned (i.e., "listen with the intention to understand") versus traits that may be innate (i.e., "be charismatic"). *Ask: Can this behavior be improved through awareness, intention, and practice?*
- **Actionable at all levels:** Choose behaviors that can be demonstrated by individual contributors, supervisors, and higher-level leaders. *Ask: Is this something everyone can take responsibility for in some form?*
- **Addresses current pain points and realities:** Values are timeless, but behaviors are contextual. Choose behaviors that address *today's* cultural gaps. Know you can revisit your list of behaviors annually or every few years as the organization progresses in its cultural maturity. *Ask: What behaviors are creating friction, distrust, or poor performance right now?*
- **Specific enough for accountability:** Prioritized behaviors should be unambiguous and non-negotiable. Avoid vague guidance like "communicate better." *Ask: Would two different teams interpret this the same way?*

Identifying Desired Experiences

The last step in defining desired culture is identifying some of the most important experiences you want people to have as a result of working in alignment with core values through observable behaviors. This is actually the whole point of values and behaviors—to create the conditions where more people are having thoughts, perceptions, feelings, and experiences that both strengthen culture and are a *result* of an intentional, thriving culture.

"Felt" experiences and perceptions are what many employee engagement and culture surveys try to measure. Consider common statements employees are asked to rate such as: "Our organization values diversity," "I trust my leader," and "My team collaborates well together." Despite good intentions, most surveys and feedback mechanisms fall short. There are typical challenges with engagement and climate surveys you'll want to avoid. As you identify desired experiences, consider the following criteria:

- ☐ **First-person, lived experience statements:** State desired experiences in "unarguable" language[3] in ways that capture the *felt* experience, not the concept. Only ask people to rate experiences they are individually having rather than asking them to evaluate things they cannot know, such as how other people feel or what the organization as a whole values or is doing. For example: "I feel safe bringing concerns to my leader without fear of negative consequences" instead of "Our organization is psychologically safe." Other examples:

Unarguable Language	Debatable or Not Knowable
I feel my leader values and appreciates me for who I authentically am.	My leader values inclusivity.
When I make a mistake, I feel safe admitting it to most of my colleagues.	Mistakes are treated as learning opportunities.
Overall, I am proud of our team's resilience in the face of setbacks.	My organization is resilient.

- ☐ **Specific language:** Name specific thoughts, feelings, or experiences rather than using vague language. For example: "I feel energized and optimistic after most conversations with my leader" versus "Our meetings are positive."
- ☐ **Within our control or influence:** Avoid identifying desired experiences that are dependent on external factors and actors such as customers, the economy, etc. For example: "I feel prepared and supported to do my job well" versus "Customers always appreciate us."
- ☐ **Aspirational but achievable:** Desired experiences should inspire and stretch people but not cross into fantasy or perfectionism. For example: "Most weeks, I feel aligned with my team on priorities" versus "We are aligned 100% of the time."

- ☐ **Future-oriented but grounded in present clues:** *Ask: Can we imagine a moment in our current reality where this has happened, even briefly?* If not, this may be too aspirational an experience for right now.
- ☐ **Written as positive presence, not the absence of a problem:** For example, "I feel my leader trusts me to manage my work with the degree of autonomy I have earned" versus "I don't feel micromanaged."
- ☐ **Avoid complicated language and jargon:** If you can't imagine yourself actually saying these words out loud to another person without feeling odd, consider rewriting. For example, "Most of the time, I feel I really belong on my team" versus "Our culture promotes belonging."

Sample Company's Desired Culture

Here's a sample of how an organization's desired future culture might be defined after a thoughtful process of discovery and conversation. If, when you read this sample, you wonder "How did they get here?" visit our website for detailed instructions and a worksheet. (See the callout box at the end of this chapter.)

Sample Company

Desired Workplace Culture

We define our desired culture with a purposeful set of core values, supportive behaviors, and felt experiences.

1. Sample Company's Three Core Values

Values define what is most important to us in terms of how we relate with each other. When we're truly working in alignment with these values, we think about them often and use them to guide our daily actions, especially when we are uncertain, emotionally triggered, or facing a difficult decision. Working in alignment with core values requires clarity, prioritization, and sacrifice.

Value	Definition
Inclusion	We do our best to ensure our thinking, behaviors, policies, and processes increase the chances that others will feel valued and appreciated for who they authentically are.
Collaboration	We work together openly, leveraging diverse perspectives and skills to achieve shared goals.
Grit	We persist through challenges and willingly embrace deliberate practice to learn and improve along the way.

2. Supportive and Undermining Behaviors

In order to create further clarity and alignment on what these three core values mean in daily practice, we operationalize them with specific priority behaviors. We identify supportive behaviors related to each value that we commit to demonstrating and rewarding more. We identify undermining behaviors we commit to minimizing and discouraging. While the list of potential behaviors we *could* focus on is long, we *choose* to intentionally focus on these because they represent what's most important to our organization at this point in our journey.

Value	Supportive Behaviors	Undermining Behaviors
	These behaviors demonstrate us working *in alignment* with our values, even when it's hard. We do our Me Work and We Work so we can more frequently demonstrate these ourselves and reward them in each other.	These behaviors demonstrate us working *out of alignment* with our values. We do our Me Work and We Work to minimize the behaviors, holding ourselves and others to a higher standard.

Inclusion	1. Listen and speak with the intention to learn and connect. 2. Invite and consider input from people from diverse roles and backgrounds. 3. When we observe behaviors, policies, or processes that may make people feel excluded, share our concerns candidly with care.	1. Listen and speak with the intention to prove or protect. 2. For input and feedback, go first and most frequently to people we are most familiar or aligned with. 3. When we observe behaviors, policies, or processes that may make people feel excluded, talk *about* people behind their back instead of speaking directly to them.
Collaboration	1. Share information freely when it is ours to share. 2. Invite input early rather than at the end of a project. 3. Practice reducing Identity Friction so Idea Friction can be fully leveraged.	1. Withhold information that others need. 2. Make important decisions in isolation. 3. Take things personally or resist others' ideas when they trigger Identity Friction.
Grit	1. Practice emotional regulation strategies to stay resilient under pressure or after setbacks. 2. Actively seek support from others during hard times. 3. Admit mistakes and share learnings publicly.	1. React aggressively toward others or emotionally shut down in high pressure situations or after setbacks. 2. Navigate difficult situations in isolation. 3. Stay quiet about mistakes and challenges.

3. Employee Experiences

While we wish for a wide variety of positive experiences for all our employees, we prioritize those we feel are *most important* to employees and the organization at this point in our journey. We'll know we're working in alignment with our desired culture when more employees report these experiences consistently:

1. I believe that my leader values me for who I authentically am.
2. I believe that the majority of the colleagues on my team value and appreciate me for who I authentically am.
3. I feel safe asking my leader for help.
4. I feel safe asking the majority of the colleagues on my team for help.
5. I feel safe admitting mistakes to my leader.
6. I feel safe admitting mistakes to the majority of my colleagues on my team.
7. My ideas are welcomed on my team.
8. I feel proud of the way our work team collaborates with each other.
9. I feel proud of the way our team collaborates with other teams in the organization.
10. With my leader, I feel safe offering a dissenting opinion or challenging the status quo.
11. With the majority of the colleagues on my team, I feel safe offering a dissenting opinion or challenging the status quo.
12. On my team, I observe people from different backgrounds working together effectively.
13. I feel proud of the persistence and creativity my leader demonstrates when things get tough.
14. I feel proud of the persistence and creativity the majority of my colleagues demonstrate when things get tough.
15. I feel proud to work here.

This Sounds Like a Lot of Work!

It might be, at least at first. If you already have clearly defined organizational values, then the process will likely be shorter and easier because you'll just need to briefly refine those and move on from there. If your organization has none of this work completed, it may feel like a significant undertaking. But investing time and energy into defining your desired culture saves time, energy, and resources over the long term.

If it helps you feel better about it or "sell" the idea to others in your company, you might think about this process as analogous to other time-intensive efforts organizations undertake in the spirit of performing at the highest level, such as annual strategic planning or budget season. Leaders routinely invest hours or even full days at a time in strategy planning sessions where they establish priorities and set goals. They do this because they know employees cannot function at their best without clear direction and a sense of where the organization is headed. The same is true for culture.

Free resources available at: www.vidlwork.com/culturejourneybook

- Sample Company's Defined Desired Culture
- Facilitator Guide for Defining Desired Culture Group Session
- CultureJourney® Guide to Assessing Baseline Culture and Progress over Time

12 The (Not So) Final Chapter

We originally planned to end this book with a chapter on how to assess baseline culture and measure progress over time. And while measuring culture truly matters, it didn't feel like the right way to leave you. Not after a book about humans, relationships, and the messy (and amazing) ways we work together. Ending in the weeds of metrics and methodology felt a little off point.

So, we made a change.

If you want clear, practical guidance on how to assess your culture (and you should), we've created a simple guide that walks through the process step by step. You can find it on our website with the other resources we've offered throughout the book. It's there when you are ready and we recommend you come back to it more than once as you lead your own CultureJourney.

Calling this the "final chapter" didn't quite feel right either.

Yes, these are the last pages of the book. But there is no final chapter when it comes to designing and nurturing a culture with intention. There is no finish line, and you're never really "done." It's a journey. One that shifts as people grow and systems evolve; one in which we expect adversity and setbacks. In the same way that strategic planning and execution is an ongoing process, workplace culture requires continual attention.

This is not to say the work doesn't get easier and smoother over time. As with any undertaking, with practice, you will develop a familiarity with the skillsets, tools, and processes necessary for attending to the cultural challenges that arise. You'll notice gaps, misses, and friction points earlier and tend to them more effectively through shared language—and with a focus on energy, connection, and courage. And you'll want to make sure you celebrate wins as you have them, even the small ones.

Before we send you forward after this (not so) final chapter, there's something important we want to acknowledge. We are culture experts, but we do not have a perfect workplace culture. We never have and we never will. Not because we don't know the work, but because culture is living, dynamic, and shaped by real humans under real pressure. For the last time: perfection isn't necessary, which is good because it's not possible. The idea that anyone "arrives" at a culture destination or culture mastery is a dangerous myth. The moment you believe you're done is usually the moment culture starts quietly unraveling.

At Vidl Work, we don't just teach language, skills, and processes related to culture. We live the work out loud, in real time, with real rewards and real consequences. And it's important that we do because our business potentially has all the ingredients for a toxic culture. We built a company rooted in difference—in people, perspective, energy, communication style, pace, and approach. We are two founders who could not be more different. You may have felt this while reading the book. Because of our different perspectives, we disagree often. We challenge each other. We see risk and opportunity through different lenses. And when adversity shows up, those differences don't soften, they intensify.

We have also grown very quickly. What started as two people bringing their individual consulting practices together has become an 11-person team providing a broad array of services requiring many different skillsets and continuous adjustment to changing circumstances.

These two ingredients—different personalities combined with rapid evolution—are notoriously taxing on relationships and can quickly undermine culture. Left unattended, the friction produced by these factors can easily become personal, defensive, and damaging. We've seen it happen in countless organizations. And we know, without question, that it could happen to us.

But it doesn't. Not because it's easy. Not because we avoid conflict. And not because we always get it right.

It happens because we return over and over again to our philosophy and our CultureJourney framework. This means sometimes we slow down when it would be easier to push through. It means we have to notice when the experience we're creating for each other no longer matches the culture we believe in.

Our purpose—to preserve and elevate human relationships as the world evolves—doesn't stop with our clients. It applies to us first. Living into our purpose means we don't get to opt out of the work when it's inconvenient. It requires continual Me Work and We Work. It asks us to pay attention, be honest with ourselves and others, repair when we miss the mark, and stay in the moment when it would be easier to disengage.

Sometimes that work is energizing.
Sometimes it's exhausting.
Often, it's both.

We've had seasons of growth and seasons of strain. Big wins and hard losses. Moments when protecting ego, avoiding sticky conversations, or letting unchecked stories harden into distance would have been easier. But our commitment to workplace culture keeps asking more of us.

Which is why this is not the final chapter of our work—or our story.

If there's one thing we hope you carry forward, it's this: The commitment to improve workplace culture is indeed a big, bold decision often involving public statements by leaders, significant changes in processes, and even much needed employee turnover. But *most* of the actual work of culture change happens in "smaller" ways—moment by moment. Do we make eye contact and say hello even though we'd rather hide behind our phone? Do we choose to ask a question and listen even when we're not sure we want to hear the answer—or assume we know and change the subject? Do we acknowledge where we missed the mark and make an effort to repair—or do we hope the person magically forgets and forgives what happened? Do we speak up again, even when it feels risky, to advocate people or problems that need attention—or do we stay quiet or give up?

Changes in workplace culture don't only happen "out there." In fact, there is no "out there" change in culture unless there has been significant "in here" change in each of us. And you—yes, YOU—have influence. No matter your role or level of positional power, if you are a human being in relationship with other human beings in your workplace, there is opportunity for you to contribute and be the catalyst for important evolutions.

Where do you start? With your everyday actions! With your Me Work and We Work.

Your Me Work: Reread Chapter 3 now that you have a deeper understanding of how important Me Work is and where it fits in the process. Reassess your development opportunities. What inner operating system updates are most necessary for you now? Where do you need to commit to evolution, adjust your thinking, or realign your actions so that you can demonstrate the best version of yourself more often? Name your Me Work out loud with at least one other trusted person—and then get the support you need to do it.

Your We Work: Reread Chapter 4 and review the We Work list again. Think closely about your team. What cultural norms exist among this group of people that you love and find valuable? Name those out loud to each other. Reward supportive behaviors when you see them. What's happening on your team that is unhelpful or unproductive? What group norms need attention? Name them—with candor and care and in the spirit of growth and development. Identify your role in the unhelpful norms, commit to your own development work, and *be* the change you want to see in others. You go first! Someone has to. Why not you?

As you finish this book, keep in mind this important point too: intellectual learning is only the first step toward change. The real work of culture change happens only when we *practice* what we've learned in this book. So we'll continue to create tools, resources, and learning pathways to support you as you move forward on your CultureJourney. And we'll continue to be inspired by the people out there like you who are making the effort, day by day, to put it into practice.

Lastly, if you're curious what it truly looks like to live this work out loud—the missteps, the repairs, the hard choices, the growth, the joys, and the rewards—just know this: we'll be walking that path ourselves and learning with you.

There is more to come. For you. For us. And yes! Eventually book number two.

Because culture work is never done. And neither are we.

Free resources available at: www.vidlwork.com/culturejourney book

- CultureJourney® Guide to Assessing Baseline Culture and Progress over Time

Notes

Chapter 1

1. Deloitte. (2025, March 24). *2025 Global Human Capital Trends: Turning tensions into triumphs—Helping leaders transform uncertainty into opportunity*. Deloitte Insights. https://www.deloitte.com/us/en/insights/topics/talent/human-capital-trends.html
2. Society for Human Resource Management. (2024, December 5). *The state of global workplace culture 2024*. https://www.shrm.org/content/dam/en/shrm/research/the-state-of-global-workplace-culture-2024.pdf
3. Sull, D. and Sull, C. (2022, September 28). *How to fix a toxic culture*. MIT Sloan Management Review. https://sloanreview.mit.edu/article/how-to-fix-a-toxic-culture/
4. Kotter, J.P. and Heskett, J.L. (1992). *Corporate Culture and Performance*. Free Press.
5. Clark, T. (2020). *The Four Stages of Psychological Safety: Defining the Path to Inclusion and Innovation*. Berrett-Koehler Publishers.

Chapter 2

1. Much gratitude to Rosie Ward, CEO of Salveo Partners, mentor, and colleague for her insights and for designing the Thriving Workplace Culture Consultant program that accelerated Rebecca's thinking.
2. Sull, D. and Sull, C. (2022, September 28). *How to fix a toxic culture*. MIT Sloan Management Review. https://sloanreview.mit.edu/article/how-to-fix-a-toxic-culture/
3. We see this truth often. Some of the clients we work with have very clearly defined organizational values that are supposed to define the desired culture and govern people's daily actions. But even when that work has been done, it is our experience that *most employees cannot state the values and do not agree that*

those values govern employee's daily decisions. Clarifying and communicating organizational values is an important starting point for culture work but does not by itself usually lead to any significant change in people's behaviors unless two additional things happen: (1) the values are further defined by congruent and incongruent behaviors, and (2) behavioral accountability is normalized to the extent that people are rewarded for demonstrating congruent behaviors and effectively discouraged from demonstrating incongruent behaviors. More on this in Chapter 11.

Chapter 3

1. Another way to think about the four dimensions of energy is this: physical energy is about the *quantity* of energy we bring to each of our moments; emotional energy is about the *quality* of energy; mental energy is where we *focus* our energy; and spiritual energy is about connecting our energy to something greater than ourselves—our life's purpose or a higher source.
2. Research indicates the most important factor in an exercise regimen for building stamina and capacity is *intensity*. Even when you don't have much time for exercise, doing a short bout of high-intensity exercises brings greater physiological and energy benefits than a longer, low-intensity bout.
3. Empathy is often misunderstood and confused with sympathy. Empathy is about leaving another person "feeling felt." It means making space for their experience or emotion with judgment, dismissal, or advice-giving. Empathy is both a feeling and a practice; it is also an incredibly helpful starting point for nearly every type of interaction or conversation.
4. The concepts of "revealing" versus "withholding" in this context come originally from the work of The Conscious Leadership group in their book *The 15 Commitments of Conscious Leadership*.
5. Kristin Neff is a thought leader in the realm of self-compassion. For more on this idea, visit www.self-compassion.org
6. Allyship refers to the practice of purposefully supporting, amplifying, and advocating for others, especially individuals who don't belong to the same social identity groups and who might have fewer life advantages or privileges than we do.
7. Heifetz, R.A. (1994). *Leadership without easy answers*. Belknap Press of Harvard University Press.
8. Clear, J. (2018). *Atomic habits: An easy & proven way to build good habits & break bad ones*. Avery.

Chapter 4

1. Clark, T. (2020). *The Four Stages of Psychological Safety: Defining the Path to Inclusion and Innovation*. Berrett-Koehler Publishers.
2. These terms are related and often interchanged but refer to two different sides of the same idea. Put simply, inclusion is more "external" and belonging is more "internal." Inclusion refers to the actions, policies, structures, behaviors, and cultural norms an organization rewards or discourages that ensure people from diverse backgrounds are invited, valued, supported, heard, and given opportunities to participate. Belonging is about the felt or subjective experience these actions achieve when people *feel* accepted, safe, seen, valued, and able to be themselves and able to contribute fully.
3. Three outstanding sources for specific language your team can rely on as you develop the practice of candor include: the concepts of "revealing" versus "withholding" from The Conscious Leadership Group's 2015 book *The 15 Commitments of Conscious Leadership;* the concepts of "rumble language" from Brene Brown's 2018 book, *Dare to Lead;* and the concept of "compassionate candor" from Kim Scott's 2024 book *Radical Respect: How to Work Together Better*. You can find a link to these resources on our website.
4. Frameworks you might consider for learning more about trust include: Charles Feltman's four components of trust, first explained in Feltman's 2106 book *The Thin Book on Trust: An Essential Primer for Building Trust at Work;* and Brene Brown's BRAVING acronym, first introduced in Brown's 2017 book *Braving the Wilderness*. You can find a link to these resources on our website.
5. In our own business and with clients, we have had great success with the Level 10 Meeting framework first developed by Gino Wickman, author of *Traction* and CEO of EOS Worldwide. You can find a link to this resource on our website.

Chapter 6

1. LeaderFactor. (2024, August 13). *What to do with a toxic leader* [Audio podcast episode]. In *The Leader Factor Podcast*. https://www.leaderfactor.com/podcast/what-to-do-with-a-toxic-leader

Chapter 7

1. Our services are most effective when grounded in a deep understanding of the organization, its employees, the objectives of the work, root challenges, strengths, and gaps. For this reason, discovery conversations are a common part of our practice. Discovery can include: a review of existing data, 1:1 listening sessions (such as with the team described in this chapter), or small group facilitated conversations, or both. Individual and group discovery conversations provide qualitative insights that surveys or organizational data might not capture and also allow us to begin to build rapport and trust with the people we'll be working with.
2. Rogers, C.R. (1954). Toward a theory of creativity. *ETC: A Review of General Semantics* 11: 249–260.
3. McGregor, D. (1960). *The Human Side of Enterprise*. McGraw-Hill.
4. Schein, E.H. and Bennis, W.G. (1965). *Personal and Organizational Change Through Group Methods*. Wiley.
5. Kahn, W.A. (1990). Psychological conditions of personal engagement and disengagement at work. *Academy of Management Journal* 33 (4): 692–724. https://doi.org/10.5465/256287
6. Edmondson, A.C. (1999). Psychological safety and learning behavior in work teams. *Administrative Science Quarterly* 44 (2): 350–383. JSTOR, https://doi.org/10.2307/2666999
7. Duhigg, Charles. "What Google Learned from Its Quest to Build the Perfect Team." The New York Times Magazine, 28 Feb 2016.
8. Clark, Timothy R. "What Psychological Safety Is Not." Forbes, 21 June 2021, https://www.forbes.com/sites/timothyclark/2021/06/21/what-psychological-safety-is-not/
9. Edmondson, A.C. (2018). *The Fearless Organization: Creating Psychological Safety in the Workplace for Learning, Innovation, and Growth*. John Wiley & Sons.
10. Clark, T. (2020). *The Four Stages of Psychological Safety: Defining the Path to Inclusion and Innovation*. Berrett-Koehler Publishers.
11. You can find a list of powerful questions to use in various scenarios on our website.

Chapter 8

1. Dethmer, J., Chapman, D., and Klemp, K. (2015). *The 15 Commitments of Conscious Leadership: A New Paradigm for Sustainable Success*. Conscious Leadership Group.

Chapter 10

1. Much gratitude to Michelle for this and many other wise observations.
2. Collins, J. (2001). *Good to Great: Why Some Companies Make the Leap. . . and Others Don't*. New York: HarperBusiness.
3. Wickman, G. (2007). *Traction: Get a Grip on Your Business*. Dallas: BenBella Books.
4. The most effective tool we've ever seen for determining whether a person is in the right seat comes for the Entrepreneurial Operating System (EOS). You can learn more about the EOS Get it-Want it-Can do it (GWC) framework at www.eosworldwide.com or through the *Traction* book, cited in note 3.
5. This point deserves repeating. This is perhaps the biggest barrier to a thriving culture we see across the board. It's common for leaders to allow "high performers" to stay in their roles even though they undermine culture, often for years. No amount of training, coaching, and consulting can overcome the damage done by a "wrong person" left unaddressed in the organization. Some of the most impactful work we do around culture involves helping leaders see this truth and decide to remedy these situations with focused accountability or removing people from an organization who do not align with values.

Chapter 11

1. Sull, Donald; Turconi, Stefano; Sull, Charles. "When It Comes to Culture, Does Your Company Walk the Talk?" *MIT Sloan Management Review*, 21 July 2020. Available at: https://sloanreview.mit.edu/article/when-it-comes-to-culture-does-your-company-walk-the-talk/ (accessed 11 May 2025).
2. SmallBusiness.co.uk. "Organisations – Vision, Values: How They Differ And Why They Matter." SmallBusiness.co.uk, 2018, https://smallbusiness.co.uk/organisations-vision-values-2542944/ (accessed 11 Nov 2025).
3. See 8 for detail on the concept of unarguable language.

Acknowledgments

It used to be that when I (Rebecca) read the acknowledgments section in other authors' books, I wondered, *How does the author have such a long list of people to thank?!* Now I understand.

It's not just that writing and producing a book requires the efforts and talents of many people. It's that the conversations and experiences that make writing a book possible unfold over years—or even decades—through interactions with people who inspire us, challenge us, and encourage us. It's also that writing a book is rarely the only thing someone is doing in their professional life. It's often layered on top of the daily grind, requiring extra time and energy borrowed from other people and responsibilities. For all of that, we have many people to thank.

It used to be that when I (Natalie) got to the acknowledgments section of a book, I skipped it entirely. Not because I'm heartless, but because I rarely know anyone and they often seem longer than necessary. I can remember *starting* acknowledgments from authors I know, fully intending to read every word . . . and then slowly realizing I was bored, mildly confused, and wondering if it was socially acceptable to just skip it. So, here's my hope today: that you'll actually read our acknowledgments. And even if you don't know a single person, you'll find at least one moment that makes you smile. Because unlike most acknowledgments I've avoided over the years, these names aren't just a list, they represent real relationships and real people who made this journey possible in ways both big and small.

Together, we (Natalie and Rebecca) would like to thank:

- **Wiley Publishing**, especially Leah Zarra for asking all the right questions and Julie Kerr for her editorial support.
- **Our "in-house" team**, Hali Grantham and Tuesday Saumell, for taking care of the inner workings of the company with unwavering dedication and attention to detail. We would be a mess without you.

- **Our client-facing team of facilitators and coaches**—Lizi Oceransky, Lorraine Williams, Luca Richards, Michelle Spehr, Shonda Kohloff, and Tod Creneti—for your patience as we grow, and for your wide-ranging contributions and deep dedication to one another and to our clients.
- **Our graphic designer, Jesse Pales**, who is quite literally the most talented person either of us has ever met.
- **Our dear friend and colleague, Stacy Bick**, for several years of time and energy that elevated our company's brand and positioned us for the next chapter.
- **James Simons aka Jim**, an incredibly gifted business consultant who helps us clarify and simplify our thinking in every single conversation.
- **Brenda Loube**, for her generosity, vision, and belief in us and the business, even before it was official.

I (Rebecca) would like to thank:

- **My parents and stepparents—Susan Johnson and James Allen, and Rodney Johnson and Doris Mathias**—for a lifetime of support that always made me feel I could do whatever I wanted if I put my mind to it.
- **My husband, Dave**, who lightens my load with humor and love—and regularly reminds us not to take ourselves too seriously.
- **My biological children, Sophia and Austin**, for bringing instantaneous meaning and purpose to my life the moment they were born, and for tolerating my "anxious pursuit of love and connection," even when it drives them nuts.
- **My stepchildren, August and Kate**, who welcomed me into their lives at the ages of 17 and 12—and with whom I get to experience the joy of mothering with freedom.
- **My business partner, Natalie**, for being everything I am not, and for being the catalyst behind so many opportunities for me and our company—including the very existence of this book deal. I could not do this without you, and I wouldn't want to.

I (Natalie) would like to thank:

- **My mom and dad, Frank and Judy Sherako**, my earliest and most honest introduction to the reality of running a business. Watching them navigate uncertainty, long days, and constant responsibility taught me resilience before I knew what the word meant. They showed me what it looks like to keep going when it would be easier not to.
- **My husband, Brad**, an avid reader, a steady thinker, and the calm counterbalance to my big ideas and spontaneous momentum. I could not do this work or live this life without you.
- **My sons, CJ and Evan**, you've made it clear since about 4th grade that reading books is not your preferred hobby, and I respect the commitment you've shown to that stance. My hope is that one day you'll pick this one up and find something that surprises you. More importantly you have given me purpose and perspective I could never have imagined. Everything is better because of you.
- **My daughter dog Leia**, who has unknowingly become my most reliable source of mental and emotional recovery. You don't give advice, you don't ask questions, and you think I'm great. It's ideal support.
- **My friends Barbara and Kathy**, for the unconditional support, laughter, optimism, and perfectly timed enthusiasm. Thank you for the shared understanding that we can always show up as ourselves, repeat ourselves unintentionally, and talk in circles. Our conversation has been a source of connection, grounding, and joy and I'm grateful.
- **My business partner Rebecca (aka Becky)**, this book, this business, and this partnership exist because of the space we create for each other to be exactly who we are. I truly could not do this without you, and I wouldn't want to.

About the Authors

Rebecca Johnson is a co-founder of Vidl Work. She oversees business operations and stays heavily involved in client work, supporting leaders and teams through consulting, training, and coaching. With more than 30 years of experience in people-centered roles, she brings deep expertise grounded in real-world application. Rebecca holds a master's degree in Counseling Education and multiple professional certifications that inform her practical, evidence-based approach. She is known for her grounded presence, her ability to translate complex ideas into usable action, and her skill in guiding courageous conversations. Rebecca lives on the West Coast of Florida with her husband, Dave, and their four children. Outside of work, she is energized by books, podcasts, yoga, running, nature, and time with her family.

Natalie Johnson is a co-founder of Vidl Work. She oversees business development, partnerships, strategy, and innovation while working with clients on keynotes, consulting, training, and coaching. With more than 30 years of experience in human performance, resilience, and leadership, she brings a deeply practical and human-centered approach to culture change. Natalie holds a master's degree in Wellness Promotion and is an industry recognized Performance Coach, sought-after keynote speaker, Certified Dare to Lead™ Facilitator, and Wellcoaches® Certified Coach. She is known for her engaging presence, big picture thinking, and her ability to help people align everyday choices with purpose and values. Natalie lives on the west coast of Florida with her husband and two sons. Outside of work, she is energized by food, travel, meaningful experiences, and conversations that spark ideas—usually more than one at a time.

Index

R

S

T